A Kabbalistic view on science

Mike Bais

A Kabbalistic view on science
Written by Mike Bais from circle of Avalon- school for Kabbalah and Western mystery tradition

Published by Circle of Avalon
Copyright © Mike Bais 2019

All diagrams produced by Mike Bais in cooperation with Vormcompagnie and with kind permission of Zév ben Shimon Halevi (Kabbalah society)
Front cover picture: Joyce Sterrenberg

The moral right of the author has been asserted

All rights reserved.
No part in this book may be reproduced, stored in a retrieval system or transmitted in any form or by any means without prior permission in writing of the publisher, nor be circulated in any form of binding or cover, other than that in which it is published and without a similar condition including this condition being imposed on the subsequent purchaser.

ISBN: 978-90-829990-0-6

Contact the author: mike@circleofavalon.nl

Dedication
To the Holy One Who has revealed Itself throughout existence in all its Splendor and Beauty.

Contents:

Acknowledgements		6
Preface		6
Prologue		7
Part 1:	Biology in the micro and macro-world	9
	Introduction: A book of life	
Chapter 01:	The senses and the world	15
Chapter 02:	The cell and the Tree of Life	19
Chapter 03:	The membrane	25
Chapter 04:	Perception controls behaviour	29
Chapter 05:	Placebo and nocebo	31
Chapter 06:	DNA and RNA	43
Chapter 07:	Memory	47
Chapter 08:	The world of Assiah as a mirror	55
Chapter 09:	Perceptions	61
Chapter 10:	Changes and consequences	67
Chapter 11:	Kabbalah in practice	71
Chapter 12:	Programmed for life	79
Part 2:	Quantum Physics	83
	Introduction: Quantum physics	
Chapter 13:	The causal ability of consciousness within the soul	87
Chapter 14:	Quantum physics and creation	93
Chapter 15:	Supramental and archetypal	95
Chapter 16:	Four Worlds	99
Chapter 17:	Soul and reincarnation	103
Chapter 18:	Purpose	107
Chapter 19:	Wholeness	113
Chapter 20:	Yesod as a mirror	117
Conclusion		119

Acknowledgements

I would like to thank all who have encouraged me to write this book: Z'ev ben Shimon Halevi my Kabbalah teacher in this tradition, Dennis Agterberg who helped me with the Kabbalistic diagrams and technical preparations, my family who always believed in me, Ramona Gault my editor and Robbert Schrover, who has checked my work and gave me many valuable suggestions.

To all the people I was privileged to teach throughout the years, from whom I learned so much.

Preface

You are holding the first book I have ever written in your hands. On my computer, there is material for maybe five books or more. I started to write this book years ago, but I was never satisfied with the process. It was never good enough, and it probably never will be. So, I learn as a Kabbalist that all processes in life have to teach us something. This book certainly did, not the least as my teacher encouraged me for some years now in the direction of writing. My attempt to cross-fertilize two beautiful and yet complicated traditions like Kabbalah and modern science is a real challenge to me. What is more important are the voices of these two traditions and how they become one voice. I would like to take you into this world where mysticism and physical science blend together.

Prologue

We all live in the physical world when being born. On this planet and in this body, we perform many actions and tasks. Classical biology and physics explain many of these phenomena in their fields of expertise. Kabbalah has described the same world of living beings, matter, and the senses as a particular expression of Divinity: the world of action. Besides the fact that both traditions talk about the same reality, they are coming in closer proximity, as consciousness and matter are brought together as two sides of the same life. This growing synthesis has far-reaching consequences for us as human beings, how we see ourselves, and what responsibilities we have. Kabbalah has taught us over many centuries that the human being has all the worlds within him-herself. Epigenetics, quantum physics, and all that comes forth out of this research tell the same story, each in its own way.

I have a scientific and medical background and have been a teacher in the Kabbalah Society for many years. I have seen the parallels between science and Kabbalah, a place where two worlds meet, and I wish to create a bridge to bring these together.

The Toledano Kabbalah tradition is alive as it grows, adapts, and integrates the old into the new. The scientific topics discussed in this book were not originally researched in relation to Kabbalah. Both the tradition of Kabbalah and the scientific tradition are paths that lead on to new discoveries. The last word has not been spoken about these sources of knowledge. The book you are holding now is both an adventure and an exploration.

This world, the universe, and all that lives in it have been called forth, created, formed, and made in a design that knows no coincidence or mistakes. So take out your Kabbalistic microscope and let us go into that world together.

Here our journey begins.

PART 1 - Introduction: A book of life

The Kabbalistic Tree of Life and the accompanying diagram of Jacob's ladder (diagram A) represent a mirror of existence, portrayed in four worlds. The Tree of Life is called the 32 Paths of Wisdom (Etz Chaim) and reflects not only the universe, but the human being (Adam Kadmon) in all its aspects. A macrocosm and a microcosm are different in substantial appearance, but in reflection are alike in principle and essence. The universe could therefore be called a macrocosm of the human being, who is a microcosm of the universe. The Tree of Life is the wisdom of the stars, planets, and all that make up the entire universe: seen and unseen. From an esoteric point of view, the universe is not only 'upwards' to the heavens above, but extends in all directions, including within yourself. Simultaneously, within the human body, we find cells of all kinds that contain minuscule organisms that are similar to the human bodily organs, with all corresponding functions. Each cell, from whatever specific tissue we may be discussing here, has all the same functions as the total organism, such as breathing, moving, duplication, secretion, eating, etc. This makes each cell a microcosm of the complete physical body, which is as a macrocosm to each cell. 'As above so below, so below as above' equals: 'So within, so without, so without so within'. Each part of the universe in small and greater size reflects and articulates the totality in its own specific way. The wisdom of the universe is therefore present in all expressions of life.

I would like to explain that from a Kabbalistic perspective, we regard 'life' as all things that contain consciousness. From the mineral, vegetable, animal, and from the human to the angelic and archangelic, all contain consciousness (or are contained by it). Materialistic sciences like biology understand living beings and 'life' as organic in contrast to inorganic beings and substances, which are dead. In this book, departing from a Kabbalistic tradition, we speak about 'life' as all things that were called forth out of that world of pure consciousness and unity: Aziluth.

The Hebrew name for this first world of emanation, Aziluth, can be translated as the world 'near to God'. It is this world that calls forth all the other worlds of creation, formation, and action. In that involvement of consciousness in the three lower worlds, all subtle and elementary substance is permeated by this world of first beginnings. All these worlds or realities are present within the Tree of Life. Through this, all the worlds are within you and without you. A tree as a symbol for Divine, archangelic, angelic, human, and earthly life was not chosen by accident, as nothing is in Kabbalah. The tree is an age-old symbol and metaphor, used to express the universal and the earthly worlds; the realm of gods and humanity. Besides this, it is an 'organic' symbol. Something that grows, breathes, decays, dies, etc., just like the human being and the world we are living in. The tree has always been a creature of memory, wisdom, and old age.

Parallel to the mythology of the tree, we find the mystical stories about Adam and Eve, who, according to tradition, were cast out of paradise. Heartbroken and in deep misery, they wept for the great loss of being away from the Presence of God. Expelled from Eden because they ate from the tree of 'good and evil', the consequences were theirs.

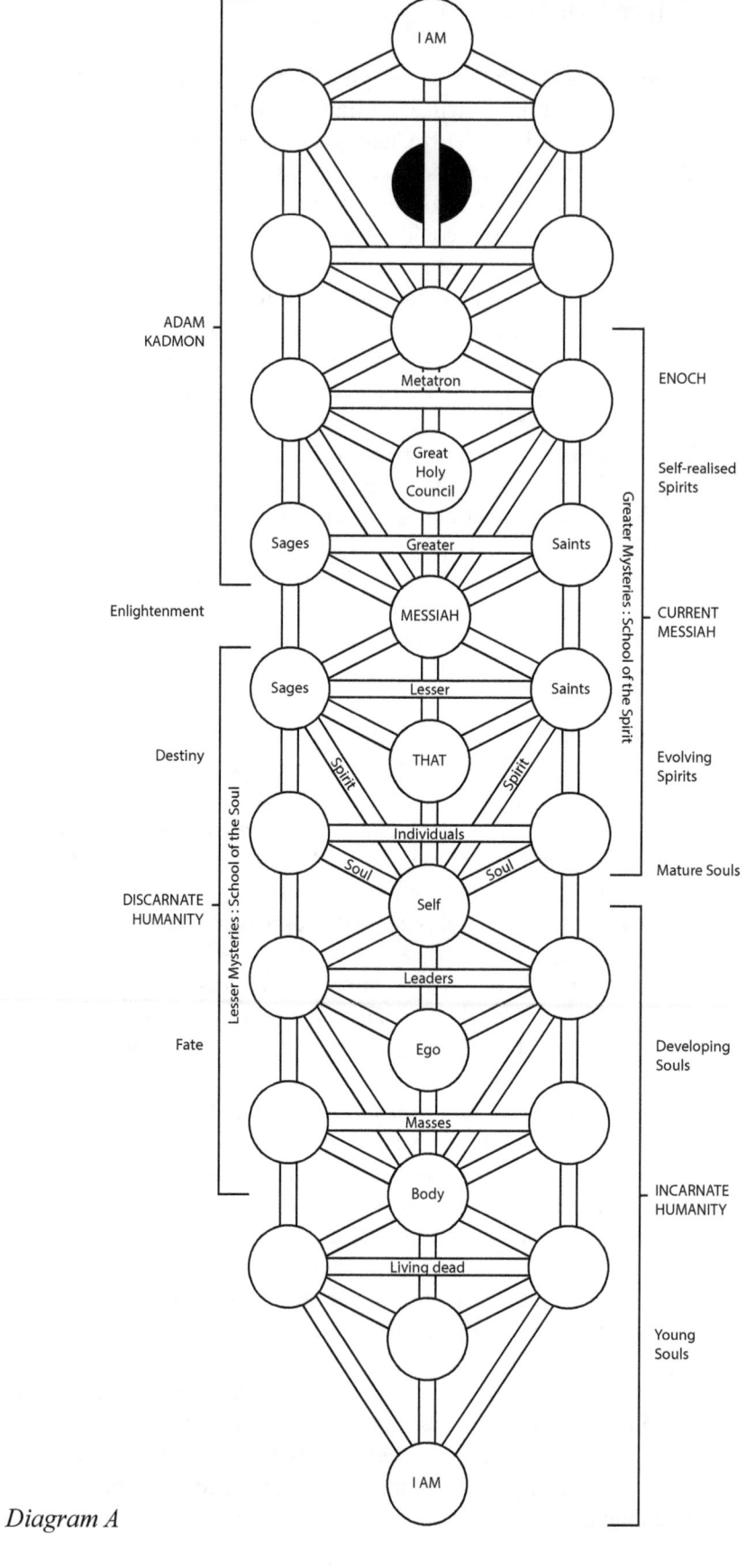

Diagram A

However, they were not left with nothing, for from that day, it was said in the book of Ratziel that every morning the great Archangel of Chocmah (wisdom) revealed the book of wisdom unto the world, for those who wish to hear.

The Nestorah Chocmah or hidden knowledge was not taken away from the world, but rather given every day, or every waking moment, to whomever wished to receive it. Let us not forget that the name Kabbalah means to 'receive', meaning not only the way of oral transmission, from mouth to ear, but the reception through the inner wisdom. That wisdom was given to humanity (Adam) when they inhabited the earth. Sepher Ratziel or the book of Ratziel is the revelation and vision of God, that the Holy One is not the secret of the universe, but that the greatest secret of mankind is him-herself. Yes, there is a mystery that lies beyond the ordinary senses, yet this mystery reveals itself continuously in all forms and energies and throughout all worlds.

This revelation was coming forth out of the heart of Aziluth, the place of the Lesser Yahweh, the great Archangel Metatron, the teacher of teachers. The movement of creation out of the Tifareth of Aziluth into the Chocmah of Briah continues into the opposite pillar, where Binah (understanding) and the principle of the Archangel Tzaphqiel lie waiting. This archangel is called the contemplation of God. Following the Tzimtzum or Lightning Flash down the Tree of Life, these are the creative 'parents' of what is yet to be created, formed, and made. The metaphysical principles of energy and form are present within these two emanations, as the uppermost part of the two side pillars of the Tree of Life. The revelation of God has now clothed itself, as it were, in the deep stillness and sanctity of Binah. The wisdom of Chocmah is received and then expressed through form, time, and space. It is through this Holy movement that wisdom becomes 'hidden' or covered in countless forms in the subtler and material worlds as the Lightning Flash descends.

As long as the Will (Kav) of God extends into the worlds, existence is nurtured and sustained. This cosmology is not of times past, but of the very moment you are reading this sentence. God reveals itself throughout nature and time-space, moment by moment, from each Now to the next.

Being born in the world of Assiah, the earthly world of physical appearance and hidden energies, we experience wisdom and understanding in mineral, vegetable, and animal form. For some souls, it is possible to see through this physical appearance, observing the underlying reality of forms. In other words, Binah reveals itself more directly, expressed in objects and substances, of which many are audibly, palpably visionary, and through smell-taste, knowable to the five senses. Still, many things that Binah reveals in the material world remain outside the understanding of human comprehension. Whether we understand metaphysical nature as it appears to us or not, the wisdom is present in every atom and molecule that make up these different physical forms and appearances.

Binah contains the wisdom of Chocmah. The Mother carries the Father in her womb. Ama is Abba incognito. Life-form expresses life-force. Life-force moves life-form.

In this book I will take you through the metaphysical building blocks of nature, where the principles of the Kabbalistic higher worlds explain themselves through readily accessible concepts. As abstract as these laws may seem, they are often more simple to grasp than our day-to-day affairs.

The whole of nature is a book of life, a testimony of the Divine that harbors all that was, is, and will be. Like a book, nature contains information that is stored in its pages, sentences, and letters. This analogy tells us that all the phenomena of the world express themselves as a 'book of life' which contains Divine consciousness in energy and form.

Likewise our human bodies carry the Divine immanence within each cell. Accepting this metaphysical idea behind nature makes our world completely different from the way we look from the lower part of our Tree of Life. In more modern terms, we could translate 'book' into 'manual' and ask ourselves, 'Have you read this manual?' Have we read the instructions of how the physical vehicle operates and functions? For most of us, the answer is 'no'. The body asks for attention through instinctive questioning to make us rest, eat, sleep, and procreate. Not much consciousness is required for these tasks. Likewise, the vital physical functions, like breathing, heartbeat, circulation, and countless others do not ask for awareness. The body goes on with its essential and vital duties nonetheless to keep everything within the body working and sustained. Even the five senses, the tools of the physical body, with which we scan and observe the world, are hardly used in a conscious manner. If we do not study the manual of the body, how can we possibly read this wonderful book of life? This book is inscribed in the atoms, molecules, tissues, organs, and complete organ system of the body.

If you ever ask your physical body, 'What can you teach me?' It is likely that it will answer, 'All you need to know!'

Vibrant, impregnated with and communicating inner wisdom, the physical body is the most reliable evidence that the physical world is like a book: it contains and receives all that comes down from the higher worlds. The wisdom is present within the DNA of each cell. Tradition tells us that Malkuth is the sphere of the physical body and the dwelling place of the Shekinah, the Presence of God on earth.

Let us start to read that book and we may discover a glimpse of the Shekinah therein.

Meditation

Sense, see, and feel your physical body, breathe through it, come to a sense of presence and Now. Be aware of the elements within the body, making up this complex organism, consisting of countless cells. These all work towards unity and harmony. Your body is the macrocosm of the cells, who are the microcosm of your body. Every cell reflects the totality of your wholeness in physicality. Now, sense and feel your skin, covering your whole body: know that this is the largest of all the organs. Through the skin, you are able to become conscious of what is inside your body and outside your body. With your eyes closed, be aware of the inside of your physical cosmos and the outside physical world. Formulate in your own experience what wisdom this brings you ...

Chapter 1: The senses and the world

The human physical body has different tools to sense the world about us. The body is constantly scanning the environment through different mediums such as light waves, auditory waves, electromagnetic waves, and chemical information. Each organism is intimately connected to its surrounding environment. We could even say that our bodies are made up of the same substances as the physical nature around us. When seeing another human being, you use the senses to primarily scan the outside features of the other person. The five senses cannot detect anything other than the physical surroundings. In other words, the senses of Malkuth are there to observe Malkuth.

'The Kingdom has five senses to observe the Kingdom'.

What is important to remember is that the senses do not discriminate between what they observe. They are simply tools for making a connection between the inner physical and the outer (exterior) physical surroundings. An organism is thus able to place itself in the physical environment and milieu. According to the experience, an organism will move towards, away from, or freeze (stagnate) in a certain environment. Behaviour comes from the interaction between inner and outer environment. This has everything to do with the perception of the world through our senses, which are the extension of the physical body. We interpret the world as we experience it, in accordance with how we have learned it to be (conditioned). That means we do not always see reality as it truly is. Even with our physical senses.

When we enter the world of Assiah (diagram B) and mainly observe what is going on at that level of Malkuth, the elementary foundation of physical life, we see that nature observes itself. As discussed in the opening paragraph of this book's introduction, even our cells possess all the same sensatory skills as the five senses of the total body. They have the same organic functions that the total body has, like breathing, secretion, reproduction, and movement. The cell is a microcosm of the complete physical body. Even more, we can say that we are a living hologram, as each part reflects the whole.

Throughout time, we have developed a perception about our own bodies, physicality, and biology. In most sciences, the body has little to do with consciousness and intelligence. In some mainstream sciences, the body was (is) regarded as a machine, with each separate part making the total machine work. We might get stuck for a long time in the perceptions of old scientists and prophets that no longer correspond with our current development and research in scientific and esoteric fields.

Darwin, neo-Darwinism, Descartes, and Isaac Newton have brought us many good things, but some ideas seem outdated and simply not true. Or at the very least, inapplicable in our present time.

Kabbalah has proven to be a living tradition over many centuries, moving with the necessities and changes of the times and places. What is often said is that religion in general and spiritual traditions are not here for humanity, but to serve Spirit.

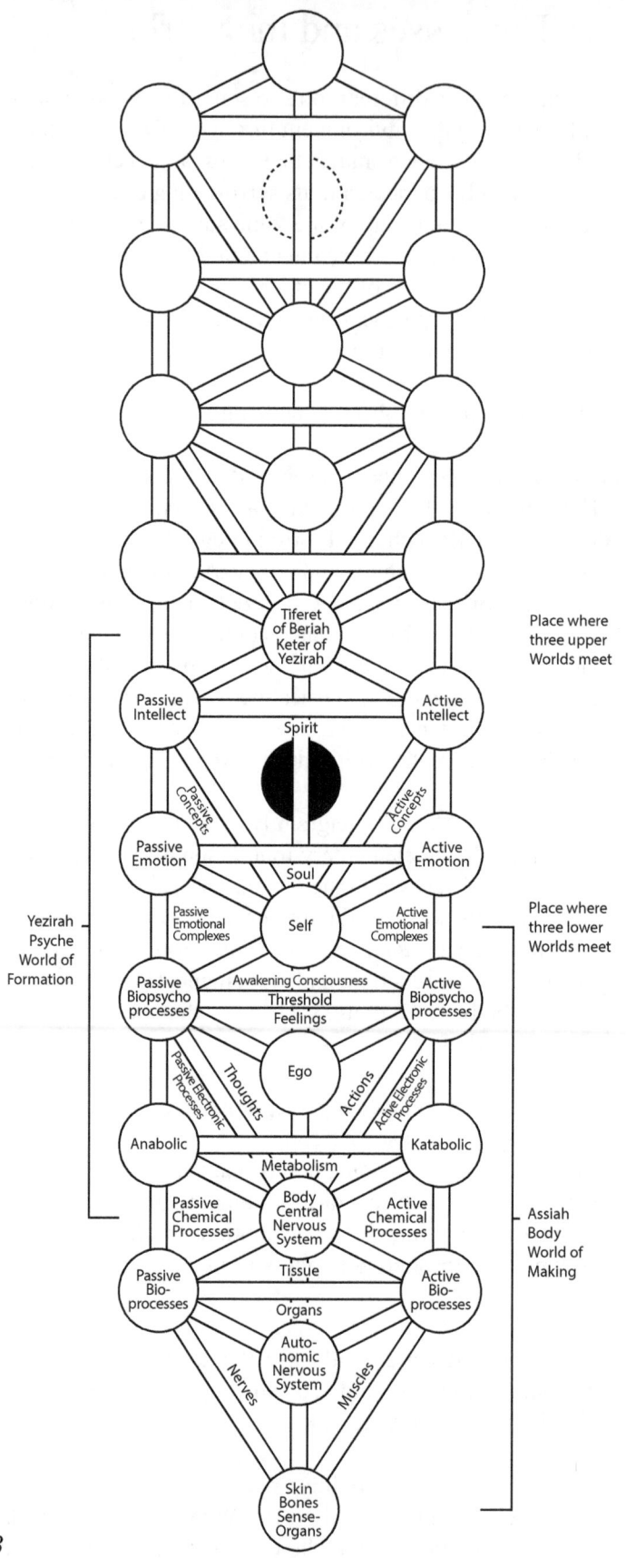

Diagram B

Humanity is not here for itself but for something greater. Likewise, the world is not here for us, we are here for the world.

Traditions in all directions of life, whether they are scientific, spiritual, or otherwise, should develop with the times, or they end up becoming fossilized and dead. A growing and living vibrant tradition needs people (souls) that carry old forms (tradition) down through the ages and develop them into a new understanding. Wisdom has shown itself throughout time by means of teachers who have promoted these metaphysical ideas about tradition and the spirit of renewal.

After all, as Kabbalists, we work with the Tree of Life, an organic symbol that is wise, growing, adapting, feeling, and evolving. Simultaneously, let us not forget that we are standing 'on the shoulders of those who have gone before'. We would not be where we are without the people who explored life through spiritual and/ or scientific means.

Let us investigate these new ideas regarding microbiology and Kabbalah.

Chapter 2: The cell and the Tree of Life

We start at the very center of the functional world of the physical body: the core of the cell. The core or center of something is often seen in the physical 'middle' of objects. But is this really true? Is the center always in the middle of a physical object? In the center of the cell (whatever physical cell we are talking about) we see the strings of DNA and the genes within the nucleus. These were/are regarded as the 'brains' of the cell. For centuries the nucleus had the reputation of being the control tower of the cell, regulating and directing all its processes. Through analogy, the regulating system in the body is the central nervous system. In Kabbalah, the function of the central nervous system and the brain is situated in the Tifareth of the world of Assiah and the Malkuth of the Yezirah. To be specific about this: the physical brain is the Malkuth of Malkuth, but its function is at the Tifareth of Assiah. The function of the autonomic nervous system lies in Yesod of Assiah.

So, here we have a cell with its physical, existential part in Malkuth. In the cell itself, we see many different 'sub-organs', performing all the life functions that the whole body as an organism is performing. According to some hypotheses, the brain (central nervous system) of the cell is in the deoxyribonucleic acid (DNA), and each cell has an equal amount of DNA. DNA has the capacity to 'orchestrate' organic functions, being the carrier of hereditary information. This information in the nucleus of each cell is said to direct and regulate the processes in the cell itself. It is comparable to the brain in the physical body. To remove the brain from any organism causes complete dis-function of all organs and reflexes, leading to immediate death. Secondly, DNA generates copies of itself, called ribonucleic acid (RNA), to send out information as DNA cannot move out of the cell. It needs 'clones' to perform that 'messenger' role. We could call these RNA cells Angels in Kabbalah.

An experiment was conducted by microbiologists in order to observe the change in cell behavior when the surrounding environment was altered, by testing various human cells in both petri dishes and test tubes. The organisms (organelles) in each cell were obviously reacting to the changes in the surroundings. Curious about the role of the DNA in the nucleus, they removed the nuclei from the cells. Surprisingly, the cells did not die, but continued to perform the regular functions in the same way that they had done previously. Some cells lived as long as several months without their nuclei (the supposed brain).

In addition to these surprising results, change was observed within the cells. The cells became 'demented' and started to lose their memories. They appeared to forget about reactions from the past and had to relearn who they were (identity) and their relationship with the outside world. Adding to this was the loss of the ability to learn something new. Memory is like data that can be recalled by human consciousness. The human psyche regards memory as personal, derived from the Tree of Life and Jacob's Ladder in the lower face of Yezirah, where the personal consciousness resides. It is located at the upper face of Assiah, where the body communicates its experience with that of the personal-psychological memory. The body, with Malkuth as the Sefira of the four elements in Assiah, has its own intelligence, including a particular kind of memory.

Although communication was observed from the outside to the inside of the cells and vice versa, the cells did not behave as if they had a memory or data bank anymore. The first conclusions drawn from these experiments suggested that although the nuclei contained the DNA and genes, they did not possess the capacity of directing and managing the cells.

In other words, the cells' nuclei were not their brain or control center but rather a memory database comparable to a library. In addition to this important data storage function, the genes operate like a reproduction center. RNA, which can transport information, is generated in the genes.

Rather than knowing itself through self-consciousness and the conscious processing of experiences, DNA requires interaction with its surroundings through the reflection of Yesod. In other words, DNA does not do anything by itself nor does it 'switch on or off', as it needs a stimulus (consciousness) to do so. DNA memory therefore reacts from the world of effects (Assiah).

Yesod in Assiah acts as the autonomic-vegetable nervous system and has the same function as DNA: it works through an automatic programme, waiting for instruction. As long as there is no new information, the programme does not change. This is identical to the Yesodic function on the psychological level in Yezirah, where the psyche has a certain programme and does not change without new stimulus. What is it that moves the DNA to be 'read' differently?

The answer is significant as the environment or outside world largely determines the constitution and well-being of your life. A hostile or friendly place can make you distressed or happy, respectively, as you experience different perceptions of your world. These perceptions send information through electromagnetic and chemical means into the organism and affects its functions (diagram C).

In addition to the environment having this huge influence on your genes and having an organic and interactive-interdependent relationship, it becomes interesting to note to what extent we can consciously influence the way we position ourselves within the world and how we perceive the world from the inside out. Perceptions are beliefs in human terms.

Whenever we stay under the unconscious influence of what the world (society and culture) brings to us, we are victims to our so-called hereditary state. In that case, our genes will determine our fate as was the assumption for decades. On the Tree of Life, this is the general fate which is demonstrated in the greater triad of the vegetable (unconscious) level. To become the victims of our hereditary line is equal to being victims of our belief systems, which means we do not take responsibility for our lives, but live the lives of our environment (parental influence, etc.).

Questions at this very moment might be: How do you see yourself? How do you see yourself in relation to the world?

To see yourself, you need a mirror. A physical mirror will reflect your physical body, but a psychological mirror (Yesod of Yezirah) is required to see your inner world.

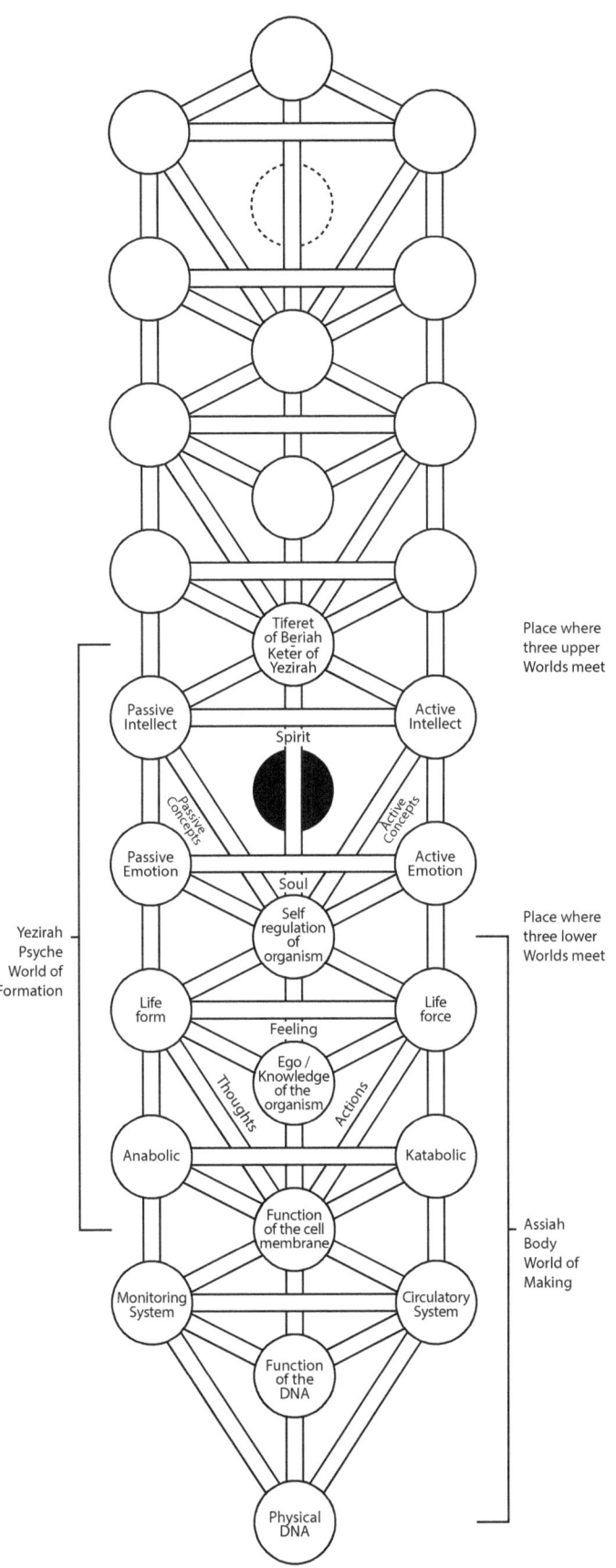

Diagram C

As DNA is a blueprint but not the final plan of the human being, the genes are in effect 'waiting' for information, for without it, they cannot move nor alter any situation in their blueprint. A gene cannot turn itself on or off; it needs input from the surrounding environment. DNA gives instruction to the body to produce proteins in the way it has learned to do so (for good or bad), and as such the organism functions. This can be explained through experiments with stem cells that are put in different laboratory conditions or environments; according to the surroundings, they evolve and grow into specific cells, like muscle, fat, or brain cells, etc.

(We could better say that the human is a 'human being and a human becoming'.)

If the surroundings were not that important and the genes were indeed completely determined by their blueprint structure, i.e., from former generations, they would utterly dictate the current affairs of our lives and we would not be able to change anything about it. Consider this in the context of second-generation postwar children who have inherited deep, traumatic influences and memories from their parents, given to them through genes, but also through behavior.

So, where is the brain in the cell? If the cell is like a machine and the brain directs everything through its genes, the genetic code is fixed and so is our life. What does that mean to free will (soul), self-consciousness, and the transformation that it may bring forth?

Meditation

Sit, relax, and bring your attention to your breathing. Become aware of all the elements in your physical body: earth, water, air, and fire. See, sense, and feel how these elements have shaped themselves into countless molecules and cells. Some are more earthy, watery, airy, or fiery, but they are all made up of the same elements. Then become aware of an intelligence within those units of life. Each cell has a beautiful geometrical and symmetrical form that expresses itself in the body you inhabit. This form is called DNA in human terms, but now see how this specific code and form changes within each cell, taking on the shape of the Tree of Life. Now, your whole body is made up of cells that are composed of the Divine diagram of the Tree of Life, where parts reflect the wholeness. Remain in this awareness for a while. Come back to your breathing, open your eyes, and bring your experience into the here and now.

Chapter 3: The membrane

Through technical developments within science, it became possible to look into the tiny little parts of the cell and commence research into the cell membrane. For centuries, the membrane was merely regarded as a simple biological frontier. There was little interest in researching the membrane, for as soon as the organisms in the cell were detected and observed with care, they became more exciting objects than the membrane. To a certain degree the skin of the body is comparable to the cell membrane—a barrier between the inner and outer biological world. Above all, the cell membrane and the skin comprise the greatest part in both the cell and the entire body. The biggest organ the human biological body contains is the skin. It allows us to have a very definite experience between the inside and outside of the physical world. Because of this, the body (Malkuth and Assiah) has a sense of what is 'me' as an identity of the biological organism and what the exterior world is, regarded as 'not me'.

Take the example of a needle when you have to receive an injection. The needle is not part of your biological identity and is rejected as outside material and 'not me'. Even natural substances, like a thorn that punctures your skin, are experienced as something not belonging to you and must be removed. The skin of the human body has the ability to feel, being sensitive to many different kinds of tactile stimuli. Consider this in the context of the five senses in the physical world: sight, hearing, smell, taste, and touch, at least for those organisms that carry all five. Some even say that there is ultimately only one sense, one way of detecting things in the environment, and that is by touch. Think about it. The eye 'touches' light when light palpates the retina, sound waves 'touch' the eardrum, and likewise with smell and taste. Nature has one sense: touch.

This sense of touch is far greater than that which we can achieve with our hands and fingers. The whole skin touches and palpates as a single organ. Through both the hairs on the skin and the free nerve endings within the skin, we are receptive to temperature, pain, and countless different impulses.

But that is not the whole story, for the skin covers not only the outside of the organism, but also the inside. Here the skin performs the same functions as on the outside. We may agree with the many scientists who, over the years, considered that the more 'complicated' organs, such as the liver, kidneys, and heart, are more interesting and important than the skin. However, it is not so difficult to see now that the skin is a truly sophisticated organ with multiple functions.

Here we have an analogy between the cell membrane and the skin. They both touch and feel the inside and outside environments. In the example of the cell membrane, there is more to it in addition to the ability to touch and gather information about the 'milieu interior and exterior': the membrane is able to make decisions based upon the information received.

These discoveries have led to the cell membrane being considered as the real brain-like part of the cell. It acts as the 'heart' of the cell, operating as a central nervous system, regulating all processes. These include harmonizing, directing,

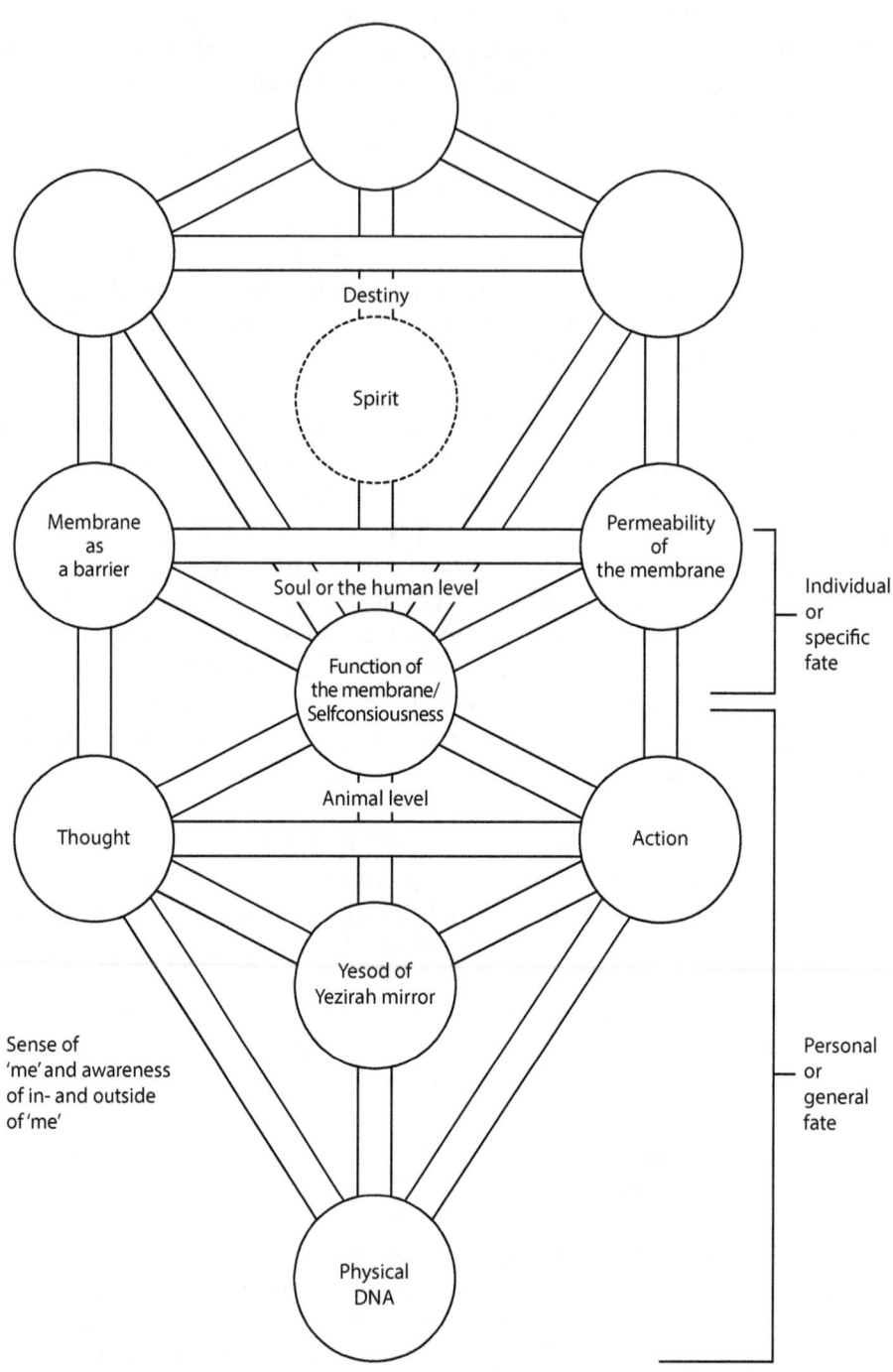

Diagram D

and redirecting the input and output of the cell. In addition, the membrane can sense the difference between the inside and outside of the cell, even having the intrinsic ability to have a sense of 'self'.

The membrane has receptors that consist of very complicated amino acids which are able to transfer information between the inside and outside of the cell. These are like the five senses of the body. We can therefore see the membrane of the cell as the crucial component where human consciousness has an effect on the genes and the DNA (diagram C and D).

It is important to note that the genes are not changed themselves, but the way they are 'read' is different. Genes cannot alter their own blueprint, so something else has to 'move' the blueprint in order to change anything inside the gene, the amino acids, the cell, and the organism. Therefore, through 'mind' and consciousness we are able to make changes in our physiology.

Exercise

Take some time to walk outside. Become aware of what and who you meet while walking. Every encounter transmits information from outside to inside of you. Be conscious of how you interpret all this information that comes your way. Your senses detect the outside world which is processed through the mind. How does the inside world within you, your feelings, thoughts, and memories react to the outside world? Do you ever question how you react to the information coming from the outside world?

Next, be conscious of what signals you give to the outside world, coming from within you. Think about your facial expression, body language, thoughts, emotions, and feelings. What energy do you transmit to the outside world?

Try to bring the interaction between your reactions together so you are aware of what is the influence from outside to inside and from inside to outside.

Chapter 4: Perception controls behaviour

Have you ever thought about the idea that 'signals control movements'?

Consider the following: the physical body does not do anything by itself. Muscles do not move, the organs do not function, nor does any vital reaction occur, without a stimulus given to the organism. Nature in general needs the same impulses to get going. It needs signals to be animated. Whenever springtime sets in, the whole of nature, including the human body (Assiah) starts reacting to this cosmic change that we call a season. Take the time to observe the body wherever you are. There is something that has moved your body to be wherever you are at this very moment. What thoughts you have correlate with where you are and how you move. The state of your outer environment determines largely the way you react and act. If you feel happy and secure within your current environment, you will respond to it with an impulse to grow and thrive. Hostile, dangerous, or threatening impulses from outside make us stagnate, fight, or run away from the situation.

Let us have a closer look at this natural mechanism, as it will be of great influence on our current topic. Humanity continually wishes to accumulate and assimilate. Most economies are based upon this idea of accumulation and growth. We regard what we have assimilated as our own, and we think we possess it as we have accumulated it and built it up. We personify the items that we have gathered and developed. As soon as we label and categorize something, we claim ownership over it. This is a Yesod-ego way of dealing with the world in reaction to inner and outer environment perceptions of our organism. If we think 'more is better', this accumulation will turn us into a type of tumour. Where does this impulse to accumulate and grow come from? Deep down, there is still a need for survival and safety, even in the Western world, where this is no direct concern for most people.

However, our way of living, with its rhythms and peculiar pace, has become a huge pressure that unconsciously invites us to live in survival mode. Being apprehensive or even afraid to maintain what you have, particularly while you are not in need, is enough to set the survival mechanism in motion within the body. Whole societies in the Western world are arranged in such a way that people worry all the time, feeling they are not safe, mostly trying to anticipate what might happen tomorrow.

Boredom is a completely different problem, coming from a leisure-focused society, not in the sense that we are lazy, but that we spend our time with intelligence-destroying and soul-diminishing activities. Entertainment from television, computers, and iPhones is a form of technological slavery and/or addiction that leads to a passivity of mind and a deadening of creativity.

Do signals control movements? Indeed they do. In the text above we have seen how our bodies and psyches react to stimuli. It does not take a professor to figure out that certain people make use of sophisticated techniques, such as advertisements, to move the masses through impulse in a specific direction. Technology uses the modern market system to entertain us and make us pay for it. What it results in is a distraction from ourselves. Many signals come from the outside world and are imposed upon us, yet through gradual, consistent, and repetitive confrontation with these signals, they become more or less our own. As a result, we cannot discern between a motivating signal which comes from the outside and one which originates from the inside. In Kabbalah, we work towards awakening and cultivating, through the process of self-observation and meditation, the difference between what is interior and what is exterior.

This is shown on the awakening triad of the human-animal nature on the Tree of Life. Self-consciousness opens the way to start seeing what drives us and moves us and which signals we wish to follow.

How we perceive the reality around us determines how we move with the world. It is most unfortunate that we do not know how we perceive nor what we perceive.

The main functioning part of our interaction with the world is unconscious, moving along on impulse via desires, wants, dislikes, and antipathies. This is explained within Kabbalah through the lower face of the Tree of Life, where mineral and vegetable levels reside within the arena of unconscious reactions and actions. Yesod is the daily conscious monitor that processes these related interactions into a personal experience. During the course of our lives, most relations and engagement with the world are instinctive, impulsive, deterministic, and predictable within the personal consciousness of this part of the Tree of Life. You have probably noticed that I continuously repeat the interior and exterior as two distinct worlds that communicate with each other. At times there might be a glimpse of consciousness that awakens to the discernment of this process, but overall, the human unconscious prevails.

Such it is with the interior of the body, where cells are grouped together like a community, communicating, interacting, and establishing connections with their environment. One of the most interesting things to know about this process is that how we perceive the world on the macro level, with our physical body within the physical environment, is how we communicate within the interior of our cells.

Chapter 5: Placebo and nocebo

The placebo effect has been noted, defined, and implemented ever since the presence of health care and healing arts within human life. The name for placebo has changed throughout time, being variously called nature, belief, faith, and superstition.

In semi-scientific jargon, the phrase 'mind over matter' is sometimes confused with consciousness over matter. Over the last few centuries, the placebo became almost antagonistic towards modern health care and pharmacy. Evidenced-based science needs deductive proof of the effects of chemicals and substances present within medication. For die-hard scientists, there is no space for doubt or reliance on superstitious ideas for the provision of medication or therapeutic intervention. Although this viewpoint is valid, taking certain responsibility for the quality of healing intervention, there is often no space for the effects that arise from healing methods other than medical substances or therapeutic techniques. Another problem from a scientific standpoint is that placebo is not objective and cannot be proven by repeated tests, leaving the placebo effect unreliable by scientific standards.

Admittedly, the placebo is derived from a highly subjective effect that some call 'belief', leaving the complete foundation of the placebo effect based on the state of human thoughts, feelings, and actions. What we think, feel, and do (the triads around the Yesod of Yezirah), comes out of who we are, for it is said: 'Who you are is what you do and what you do is what you become'.

The placebo is at work in everybody's life without exception and even without their awareness of their participation. Most die-hard scientists believe in something, even if it is the belief that the placebo does not work! The placebo is definitely not the sole result of conscious intention or formed from the intellect and cognition. The power that is inherent in the human being, making it possible to change things, comes from the unconscious. It is neither the physical body (Assiah) nor the ordinary psyche (Yesod of Yezirah) that is capable of setting a placebo effect in motion, although these levels definitely cooperate to bring about the placebo effect. The leading factors in establishing the placebo are in fact the unconscious beliefs and conditionings that have been constructed throughout our lives, especially during childhood.

Why is it important to talk about placebo in the first place in this book? Because we are talking about processes that influence the material manifest world and the human body, through learned mechanisms, conditionings, and beliefs. In the biological theories in this book, we approached the assumption that DNA and gene constructions in the human cells are not determined or fixed units of information, but can be changed in the way we consciously interact within the world. For the Kabbalist and any inspired person who wishes to follow fate and destiny in order to grow and transform, this effect needs to be recognized. It is partly caused by the environment and structures relating to culture, religion, family, upbringing, education, friends, and work. See the Tree of Life diagram with the passive and active intellectual concepts on either side (diagram E). These triads are positioned in the upper half of the face of Yezirah and thus are the deeper psychological concepts belonging to the collective unconscious. Many

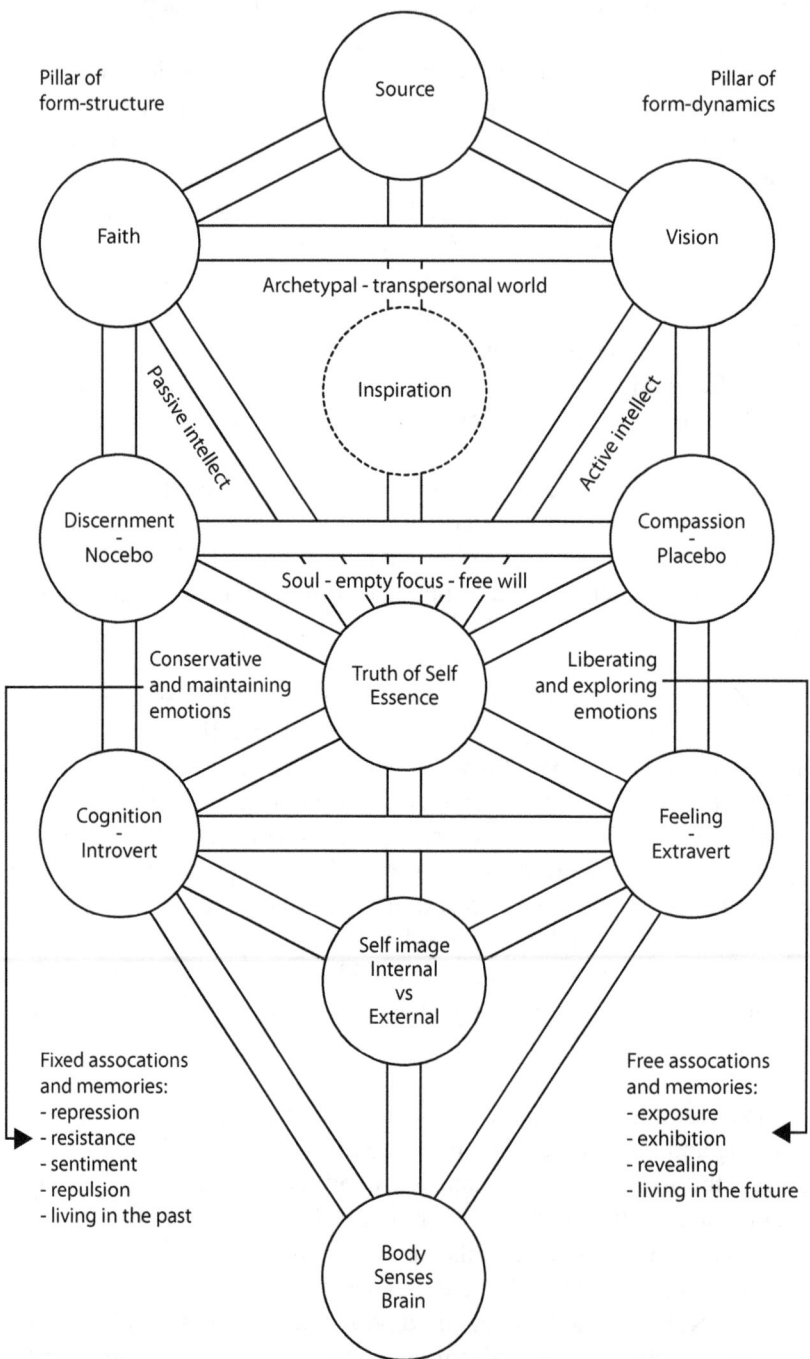

Diagram E

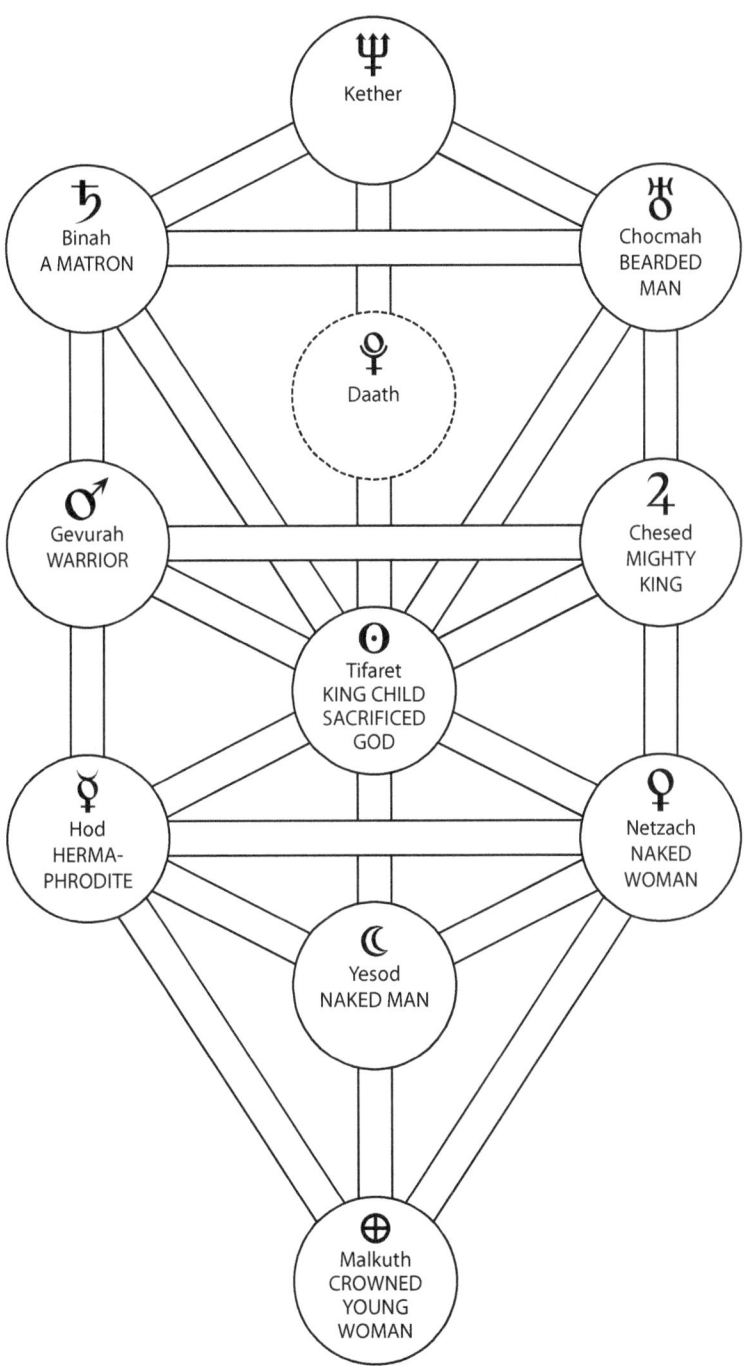

Diagram F1

specific archetypal influences are present here that affect the person at Yesod in the personal consciousness (diagram F).

The human being is moved by higher intellectual and cultural concepts. Deep emotional imprints are of great influence and are stored in the personal memory, causing all kinds of automatic actions to be operative.

The emotional triads on the Tree connect both side pillars to Tifareth of Yezirah as passive and active emotional complexes. On these levels, the person (Yesod) has little awareness in his or her daily life, merely living with the effects that these deeper, psychological levels are causing.

To what extent a person is vulnerable and sensitive to placebo is very much dependent on these deeper influences. For example, in cultures where superstition regarding religion and in folk traditions is prevalent, people are psychologically more open to placebo influences. As a rule, intellectually formed psyches do not respond easily to the placebo effect and disregard it as nonsense and superstition. Here we see the difference in the influence on the side pillars as well. The passive pillar of structure with the Sefira Hod at its base (cognition and intellect) is less open to placebo, suggestion, and subjective influences, while the right, active pillar of force, with the base of Netzach, is receptive to suggestion. Of course each human being contains both pillars, and subtle and delicate work is required to balance these two opposing and complementary principles in one's own being. However, we should not forget that in cases where the psyche is too receptive towards placebo effects, it risks falling into the trap of superstitious beliefs and naivety.

The placebo effect has a strong connection to the optimistic stance of positive thinking, which is so famous in the New Age movement of the last decades. We should remember, however, that positive thinking only works when our conscious intention is supported by our unconscious life. Our whole being, including emotions, instincts, and feelings, has to support the positive outlook on life. This means that the whole natural human being should be involved with the belief structure before anything, such as positive thoughts, might start to work. Metaphysically, the whole Tree of Assiah should be aligned with the personal belief to such an extent that it becomes a reality in the present (middle pillar). All levels should be in agreement with the belief, so that body, mind (psyche), and consciousness are operative in the process. There should be no space for doubt, like in the example where a patient receives placebo pills instead of real medication without knowing and which consequently have the same effects as the real medication. The same effect has been noted with placebo operations where the patient was told certain surgery has been done, whilst there was only an incision but no real operation. Results were nonetheless achieved for the patient, who became relieved and at times recovered completely.

Both the left and right pillars on the Tree of Life have their specific qualities and functions. They can be complementary if both force and form serve each other in the mutual recognition that they both need each other in order to exist and function. Form cannot do without force and force cannot do without form. Kabbalistically, the Sefira Malkuth is the ultimate amalgam and synthesis where

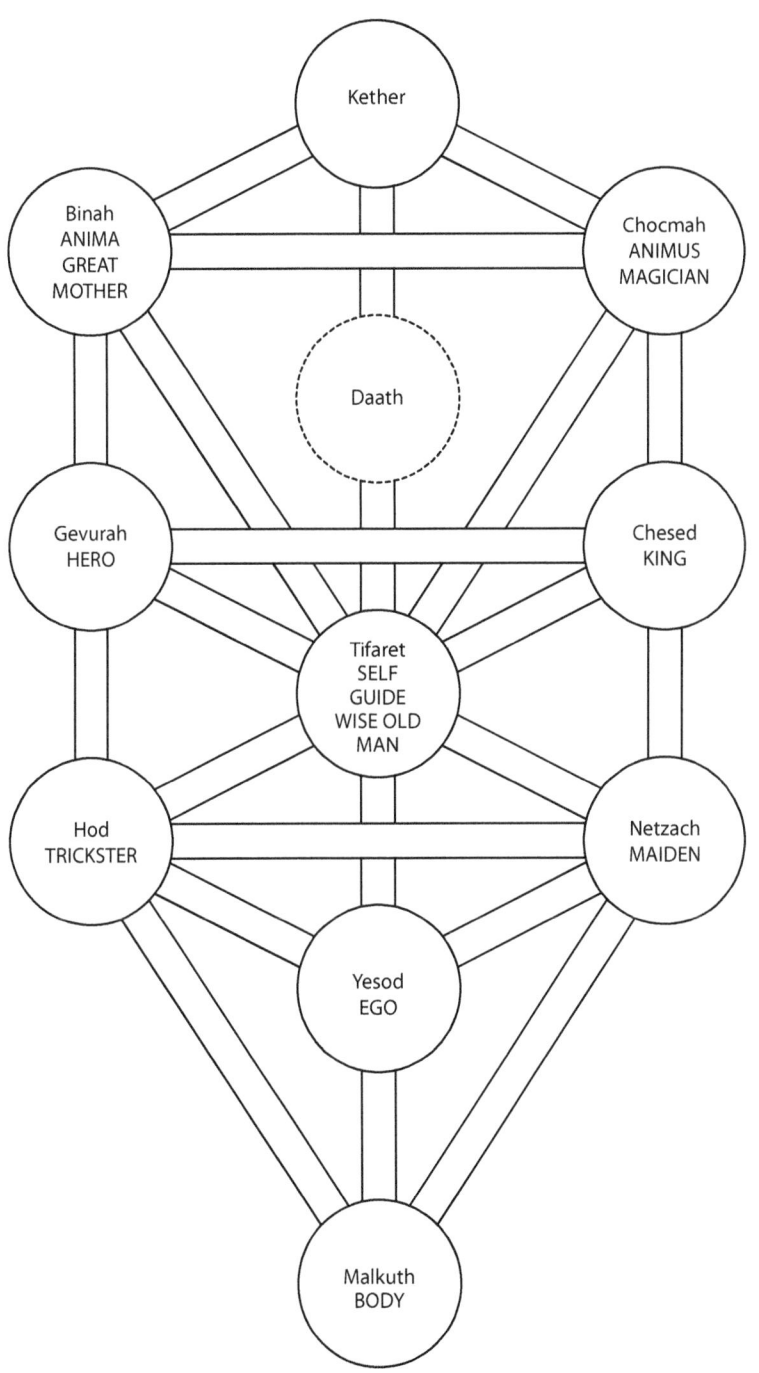

Diagram F2

force and form blend into a material vessel consisting of force-form at the base of the middle pillar. The Kingdom, Malkuth, is not only the ultimate form, as may be superficially seen and detected by the senses, but is also the ultimate force, as equally the right and left pillars materialize in Malkuth.

The placebo effect stands opposite the nocebo effect, telling the reverse tale in the human story.

As a human being is able to be very constructive and nurturing towards oneself (placebo) on the right side pillar, conversely one is also able to destroy and break one's self down (nocebo) on the left side pillar, through negative ideas, memories, and feelings.

People who are too critical and cynical towards themselves and the world have a low self-esteem, and feel unsafe in the world and within themselves generate a tendency towards the nocebo effect. The psychological mechanism remains the same in both examples: a heightened sensitivity, strong relation to outer symbols and signs, and a need for something secure. The nocebo effect arises in people and personalities that lean towards the left pillar and the emotional triad of Tifareth-Hod-Gevurah: the passive emotional complexes. These complexes are recognized by a tendency towards fear, anxiety, negativism, cynicism, nostalgia, and conservatism. These qualities should not be seen as unwanted and undesirable, as they are complementary to the right pillar on the Tree. If the cosmic Tree of Life does not balance itself out properly through subtle observation and participation with these spiritual laws, there will always be disbalance. Consider the situation where a person is emotionally inclined towards the right triangle of Tifareth-Chesed-Netzach, with poor complementary and participatory influence from the triangle on the left side. The results will be manic, hyper-euphoric, overbearing, and neurotic behaviour, through the uncompensated forces of Chesed and Netzach.

Back to the nocebo effect. As every Kabbalistic world corresponds to every other by mirroring and reflection, so does the world of Yezirah, with the emotional side triads discussed above, have its reflection in the world of Assiah, the world of action. From the world of forms, personal ideas and emotions arrange themselves and manifest into active results in the physical-elementary world. In that same triad in Assiah we see the corresponding chemicals that mirror the psychological state that existed prior to its physical counterpart. In this triad in Assiah, the triangle of Tifareth-Hod-Gevurah, we find passive chemical enzymes and hormones. Examples of these chemicals in the human body include but are not limited to low testosterone, thyroid, or adrenaline levels, and a high cortisol level and imbalance in oestrogen levels.

Another important thing to mention is the duration of the physiological imbalance of the hormone levels in the blood. Often, the longer the disharmony is present within the body, the more difficult it is to rearrange the situation through the central nervous system and autonomic nervous system present in the Tifareth and Yesod of Assiah, respectively. These two biological systems work together for the release, cooperation, and reabsorption of the above chemicals. Nocebo is known

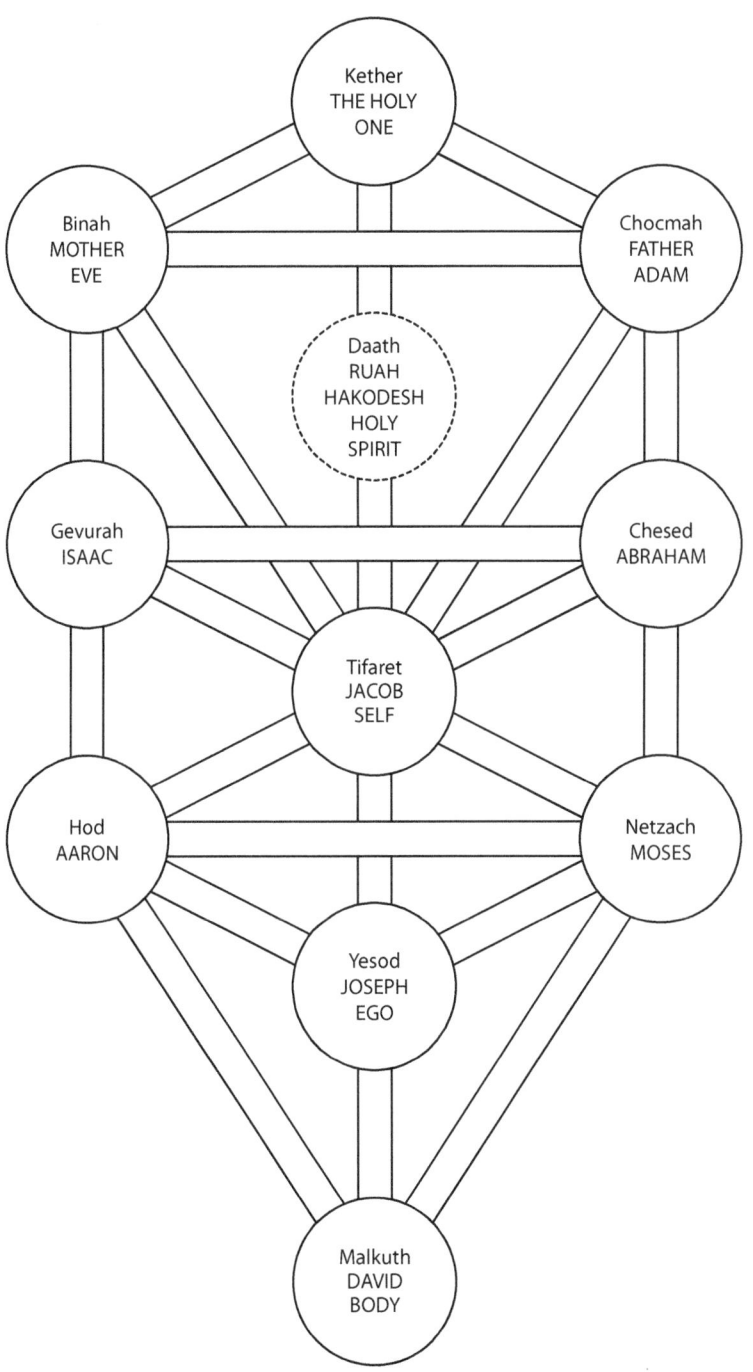

Diagram F3

and recognizable through behavior and specific 'superstitious' tendencies. For example, a person is afraid to take medication for high blood pressure. The pill is associated with the fear and anxiety that the person feels towards medication in general. Each time the person takes the pill, the chemicals of the pill are regarded as 'fear and anxiety', turning the object into a kind of negative talisman. This can evolve in such a strong way that the effect of the medication is almost or completely neutralized. The nocebo effect can be so strong that the chemical effect is completely deranged and the psychological-emotional effect is in charge.

Nocebo works also through symbols and signs. Another example of this is illustrated when a person has a negative experience (e.g., a sudden pain in the stomach) during a walk through the park. From that time on, the association is made between the location in the park and the phenomenon of pain.

There seems to be no logical explanation (Hod) between cause and effect here, but the feeling triad (Yesod-Hod-Netzach) reacts with finding an immediate reason for the stomach ache.

There has to be a reason for this fear in people who live in a mode of anxiety. If there is no correlation within the logical and intellectual domain, the 'logic' of the feelings that are dominated by fear and anxiety create pain, discomfort, and other negative sensations. The fact that there is no logic or correlation between cause and effect does not bother these people. After all, the most important thing is to have some kind of comfort coming from self-constructed correlations and experiences. Deep behind this dynamic lies the basis of the nocebo: fear and anxiety drives the human being towards the need for maximum control. If there is no control, they generate control by 'fixing' their reality with fantastic ideas within a self-made reality.

Metaphysically, the whole Tree of Assiah should be aligned with the personal belief to such an extent that it becomes a reality in the present (middle pillar). All levels should be in agreement with the belief, so that body, mind (psyche), and consciousness are operative in the process.

To be able to do this, we need the power of Yesod in order to navigate through the psychological labyrinth. However, if we do not navigate Yesod through our awakened consciousness from the animal triad (Tifareth-Hod-Netzach) or the soul (Tifareth-Gevurah-Chesed), Yesod will follow our instincts, emotions, and conditionings. There is simply no choice for those who only live from the body (Malkuth) and the ordinary psyche (Yesod) alone.

Exercise

Wholeness is making all parts connected to each other and giving them their right place and order. Use Diagram A or a diagram of the Tree of Life of your own and sit opposite it. Look at the triad of contemplation or thinking. Feel and see this triad within your own anatomy. See and feel the three Sefirot within your physical and subtle bodies. Do the same with the triads of action and devotion. Become aware that you have established the triad of the mineral and vegetable level within you. Now look at the animal triad on the Tree and see and feel this within your bodies or what we call worlds in Kabbalah. You have now actualized the lower face or garden in your own being. Become aware that these levels within you should be aligned and connected in order to make inner changes happen. Whatever good and healing thought you have at this moment, let feeling and action follow this same thought. Let your body flow with this thought, and may every initiative and movement be in accord with this thought. Rest for a moment within this experience.

Suggestions for these healing thoughts are: love, forgiveness, gratefulness, joy, friendship, or any other thought of your own.

On the Tree, the lower face contains the mineral, vegetable, and animal levels. Most of the aforementioned placebo-nocebo effects play out on these levels for better or worse. Conditionings of the biological system, along with the thoughts, feelings, and actions in the psyche, direct and orchestrate our life on individual and collective levels. The possibility to awaken these unconscious levels begins with the animal level triad of Hod-Netzach-Tifareth. In this part of the animal psyche, we become acutely aware of our biology and personality, including their contextual references and behavior. The animal triad is also called the pre-conscious triad of the animal man, with its compulsory tendencies, wakeful attention, and aspiring position on a social level. Looking at the Tree diagram, we cannot see or function above our own level of experience. The human animal can only look 'down' from this position and is only aware (awakening triad) of what is going on on those levels prior to its own development. Those are the mineral and vegetable levels (diagram G).

From the animal level and beyond, rising up the Tree in ascending order, the human consciousness can make the difference between an unconscious life and a growing, conscious-oriented life, where we can cause effects through the use of free will and consciousness. Awakening is a state, not a stage of development per se, meaning that we can enter such a state through practice or by circumstance, but also move out of it just as quickly.

For most of human consciousness, there is no sustainable and stable awareness on this restless animal level. In our biology, the interior of our cells continuously reacts to what is moving within the psychological consciousness. As stated previously, living life from the unconscious, conditioned level does not initiate any change or improvement. The only way to have an effect on the biological organism comes from the animal level and preferably beyond.

DNA and genes are not able to alter any information from within their own structure. Almost comparable to a piece of software, they operate the way they were programmed.

If that programme carries out a nocebo effect for a prolonged period of time, the DNA will accordingly structure itself, making the body arrange and rearrange data in the genes identically to the nocebo input. Of course, the same happens when we cause a placebo to take effect in our bodies. In all of this, the gene waits for instructions.

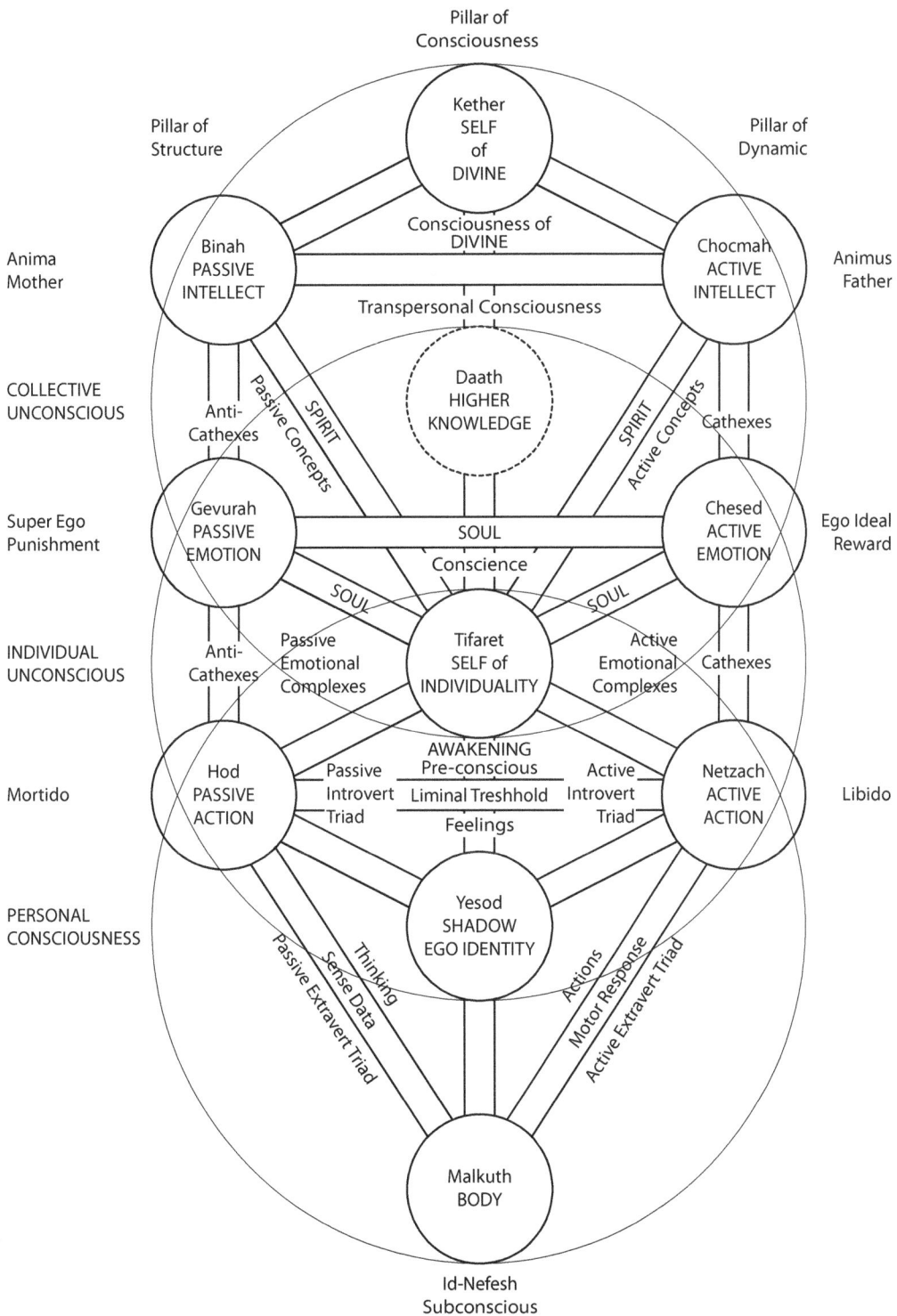

Diagram G1

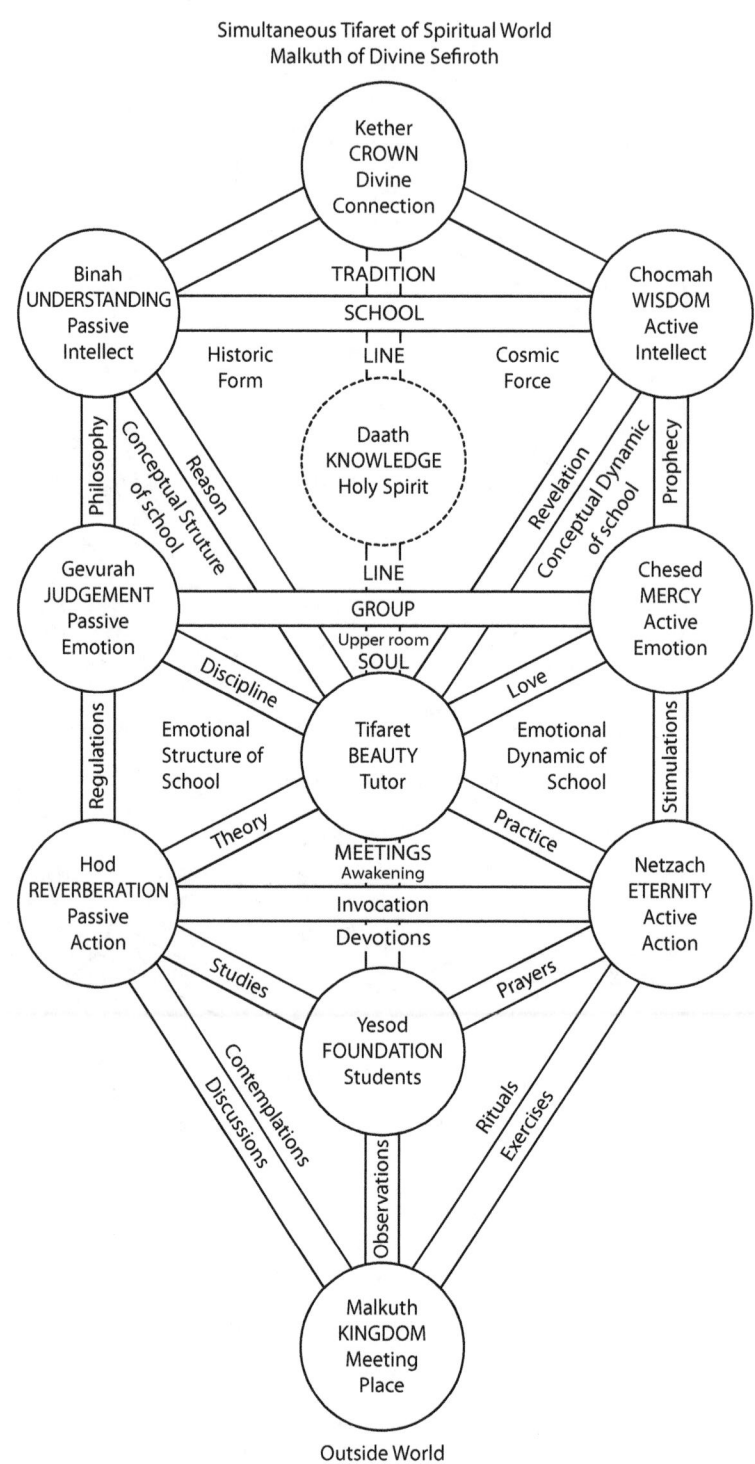

Diagram G2

Chapter 6: DNA and RNA

Without getting too deep into microbiological technicalities, we now need to discuss the way that the information in the cell nucleus, where the DNA and genes reside, moves through the interior of the cell and even beyond in the extra-cellular space. DNA is a thread-like chain carrying the genetic data and instructions used for growth, development, functioning, and even reproduction within living organisms. In each nucleus of a cell, we find two strands or 'ribbons' that store biological information. These two DNA strands of every nucleus store the same biological information. This information is replicated as a clone of information that is held within the chemical structure of DNA. This was discussed previously in chapter 2 and is called ribonucleic acid (RNA).

In Kabbalism, the double strands of the DNA structure can be seen as the Jacob's Ladder, a spiral staircase of evolution. Going up and down the ladder represents evolution and involution.

The spiritual beings who ascend and descend that Ladder of Lights represent the genes that pass on their wisdom. This was seen by Jacob in the book of Genesis, when he was asleep seeing Angels ascending and descending a ladder that reached from heaven to earth and from earth to heaven. These Angels represented whole epochs and civilizations moving in and out of existence.

RNA is a movable, mirror-like chemical structure that contains identical information to its respective DNA from which it was generated. RNA molecules are essential for various biological processes, including coding, decoding, regulation, and expression of the genes that are present in the DNA-nucleus. DNA is static in its position in or stationary within the cell, but not stationary regarding the possible changes that occur from reading information differently. RNA is the mobile equivalent of this information, sending out the identity of the cell (at that particular moment) to the environment. RNA has a messenger function, mediating between genes and the interior and exterior environment of the cell.

RNA therefore has an Angelic occupation on the microcosmic level of Malkuth. It is the messenger of the Kingdom or scout of the biological emanation of the Tree of Life. Nature as a whole continuously exchanges information within and without all kinds of species and organisms. So it is for the human being, having his/her natural life in the world of Assiah. The natural world is constantly moving as we know in Kabbalah, coming forth from the name of this world called Assiah (diagram H).

All is in motion. This is the same for each organism and the environment. Nothing will move as long as there is no exchange of information within the cell.

RNA carries countless hereditary and non-hereditary pieces of information around and through the body without our conscious knowing. It is important to remember that this kind of information refers not only to the physiological and biological aspects of nature but also to emotional thought-patterns and many other more subtle kinds of information.

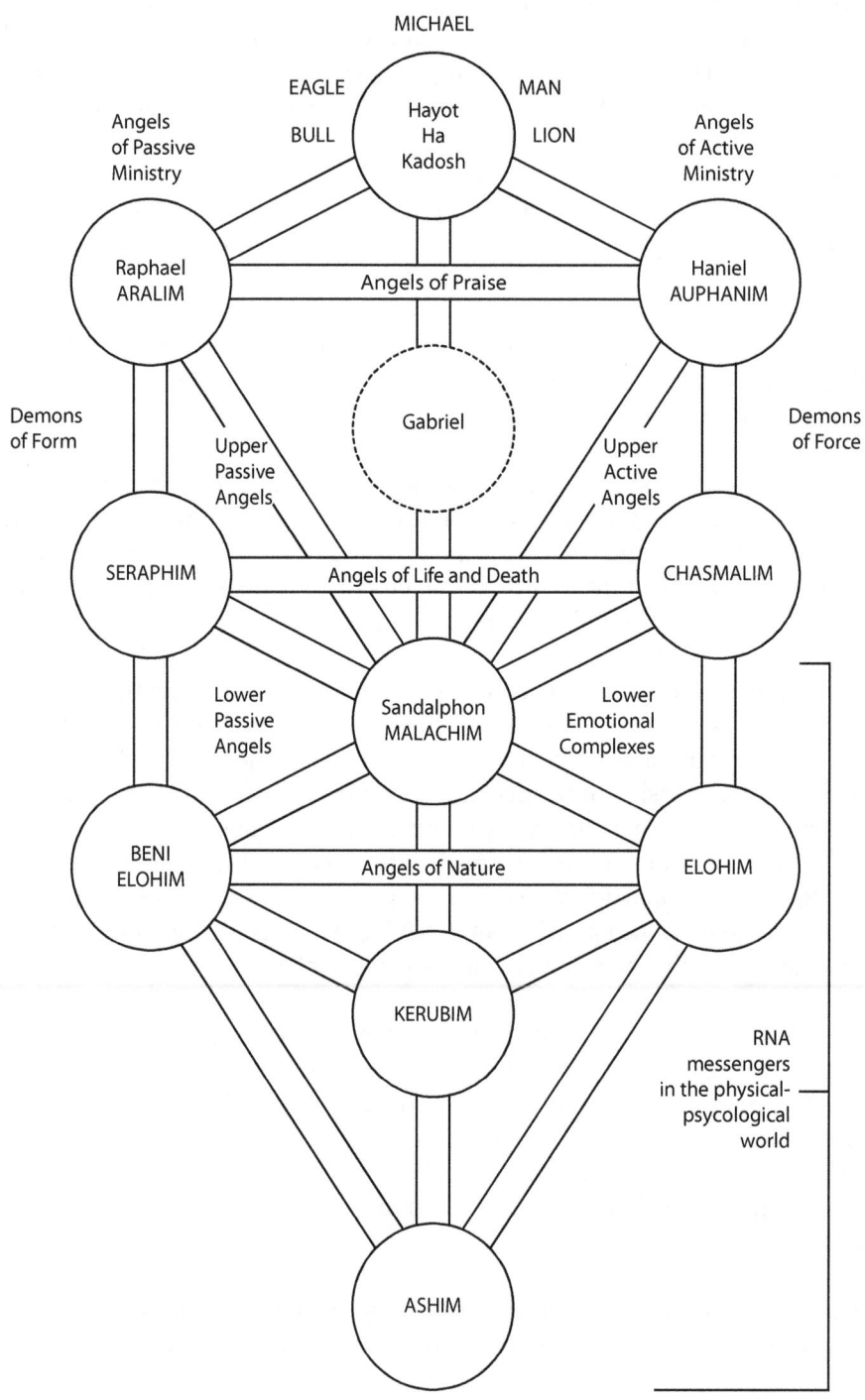

Diagram H

Each Kabbalistic world, with the exception of Aziluth, has its own kind of memory. Assiah has a biological memory that is transmitted from parents to offspring. It is present within each organism and moves in between cells, tissues, and organisms.

In Yezirah, we find a storage of memory in the etheric-astral domain, which is sometimes called the Treasure House of Images. This is located at the Yesod of Yezirah. Here we remember or re-member information that comes to us through images, symbols, and shapes. Although it is centered on the personal consciousness, we all share from this repository of collective used images which are recycled and moving through many ages and traditions.

There is memory beyond the natural and personal world, based at the Yesod of Briah: the Treasure House of Souls, where consciousness recalls spiritual or metaphysical memories of a transpersonal and transcultural nature. What we have in the three lower worlds (Assiah, Yezirah, and Briah) is a biological (physical), a psychological (personal), and a spiritual (transpersonal) memory, respectively. Although there is no memory in the world of Aziluth, the Divine is being remembered in the three lower worlds. We could therefore say that all three memories are modes of remembering Divinity in different ways. Aziluth is re-membered by coming home into the union with the sacred Shekinah at the Malkuth of Aziluth.

There is a saying in Kabbalistic tradition that forgetfulness is exile and remembrance is liberation. Meaning that to find oneself, we must come to know who we are once more, and remember this on all levels, in all worlds. This is the way of inward ascension or Teshuva, the way of return or the reverse Lightning Flash. It is said that the Holy One wishes to behold Itself in the mirror of existence. Such can only be done if the mirror is whole and clean, having been made complete by remembering and then cleansed by the inner process of truthful reflection.

I invite you within the scope of this book to move into the densest and most compact details of the physical body and to remember what has descended into the physical vehicle. Ultimately all the worlds are emanated, created, formed, and manifested within the physical universe. The world of Assiah is therefore a living synthesis of all the former worlds. In conclusion we recognise that the physical body is truly a spiritual vessel (diagram B).

Information stored in the specific physiological codes of DNA within the genes is therefore not simply biological memory, but an amalgam of influences from the descending worlds that exist prior to their manifestation in Assiah. Every cell, tissue, and organ has a voice, and what the interior of the body communicates to us through these different voices is much more than a physical aspect and describes our psychological and spiritual nature. This idea, blending physical and metaphysical nature together, radically changes the way we think about the body. This is part of the new biology.

Exercise/meditation
Sit or lie down and close your eyes. Imagine that you can see every thought that appears from within. Let all that wishes to show itself in your memory come to the surface. You may see or hear words, see images, and have corresponding feelings with them. Let all these thoughts and images come to you. What you are now gradually witnessing is the Treasure House of Images. All these images seem to belong to you, but know that they come from a vast world of memories that we can all access. A collective memory and unconscious. You may even realize because of this that all our memories originate from the same source: the Treasure House of Images.

Chapter 7: Memory

Memory does not move by itself. Information does not move by itself. However, both move by means of associations coming from the inside or outside of the body. Memory and awareness of the body come through the central nervous system at the Malkuth of Yezirah. Simultaneously, this is the Tifareth of Assiah and as such is at the heart of the physical vessel. Here is where we find the function of the physical heart. In addition to working as a muscle that pumps blood around the whole body, the heart facilitates the flow of information through countless different cells as they are transported through the body. These are the principles of cycles and flowing motion in Netzach and information coming from Hod. These principles work through Malkuth, the physical elementary body.

Yesod of Assiah, the autonomic nervous system, mirrors the status of how the complete organism is operating. From this reflected image you can sense the interior of your body. Although this level is a very rudimentary form of consciousness, the process is eventually of importance if one wishes to evolve consciously. In the Daath of Assiah/Yesod of Yezirah these experiences come together into the knowledge of the body. From this complex of Daath/Yesod, one can actually ask the body questions, which in many cases the body answers with vital responses and intelligence. That is, if one is sensitive to it from the triad of Yesod-Hod-Netzach in Yezirah (diagram G).

The physical vessel is literally a body of knowledge containing and providing knowledge on an unconscious level, but this wisdom is also accessible when it is asked questions, bringing answers to the surface of consciousness.

How does this relate to memory? Because nature in general and humans specifically function and live on very old foundations of memory, thus giving life into the hands of the unconscious.

Making no attempts to experience something beyond what one already knows, or to generate new memories, will not change anything in our biology. This highlights an important principle in many esoteric traditions, including Kabbalah. Although one might indeed ask if change in experience and memory is necessary.

The scientific-Kabbalistic development discussed within this book encourages us to know that change within the body is possible and that even the general fate of the physical organism is not fixed and its DNA is not written in stone.

Let us not forget that the way of the Kabbalist is a path towards wholeness and unity. In general, the Kabbalistic and other esoteric paths are not always about change. Spiritual work is therefore not only about change and growth, but about self-knowledge and awareness.

In the modern world, especially in the West, there is a tendency to feel that the need of doing something and becoming conscious of something is synonymous with taking action.

For the life of the mystic who participates within the world, awakening and involving oneself with an experience is something other than taking action. Becoming and being aware are sufficient to cause changes in life.

We are undergoing changes in consciousness merely by absorbing this knowledge and contemplating it. Thus, every experience within the moment of now contributes to the possibilities of making new memories and empowering or disempowering old memories. Conscious choice, in other words (free will from the level of the soul), opens up a new horizon about our personal history and how we might affect this memory if necessary. This can also preserve memories that are fruitful, nurturing, and constructive in order to support a healthy inner environment for learning.

Consider that our psychological and emotional memories are not so different from the physical memories which are all saved and stored in our DNA and genes. This entangled situation of memory in nature, where Spirit, psyche, and physicality cannot be separated, brings to us far-reaching consequences of how to use memory for deep spiritual work and healing.

Memory in esoteric teachings and Kabbalah is often seen as a reflection of knowledge coming from a universal source unknown to the physical senses. The universe is knowledge, condensed in memory that can be accessed by each individual. Through personal experience in this universe (remember that the universe is within and without), we regard these experiences as personal, while in fact, they are universal data that were there all along. There are few personal aspects with regard to the universe or the nature that surrounds us. Even our own physical body is not a personal possession, but we develop a strong personal relation to it as being 'me'. In this way, the universe becomes personalized, and on the way, we construct a collection of memories that we call our own. These personal memory banks make us units of limited yet also specific and unique experience. In the new biology, this uniqueness also expresses itself in the so-called phenotype or the way we physically appear to others. This is related to the ascendant in Kabbalistic astrology. These memories bring tendencies and conditionings with them, operating mainly from an unconscious inner life. The spiritual way towards self-consciousness is the way into the unconscious not only of the psychological world, but also of the physical world.

The function of memory seems to be directly related to karma. Human actions are mostly forthcoming from memory, conditioned reflections, and repeated patterns. Each person has their own particular complex web of memories which orchestrate emotions and thoughts that lead eventually to action. It is almost by definition that memories work through the unconscious, finding their way automatically into the physical body. Actions not only mean motoric actions, but also visceral (organic) actions that may lead towards beneficial or less positive effects in the organs.

A simple example is the hospital visit of a relative, where the sights, smells, and sounds facilitate responses coming from memories of when the visitor was in the hospital in the past. Such an event might stir up multiple psychosomatic reactions. Without awareness to accompany these reactions, one is prone to relive similar behavior, repeating over and over again the same patterns. Personal history can serve us very well, depending on the quality, related patterns to fate, and if the memories share a 'path' on which the person has set out his/her destiny.

Old memory structures may serve an old life but may be in opposition to a current one. Being aware of these memories is the pre-condition of how to let them go, or preferably to transform them.

In the example of the body, a memory is not simply a 'picture in the head', located somewhere in the temporal lobe or amygdala of the brain.

If you remember something, the whole physical body resonates and remembers the experience. Likewise, a memory in the physical body in some organ, tissue, or cell is remembered by the whole organism. The human organism can be seen as a hologram in the physical and psychological world, where each part reflects the totality and the whole. Every part of the body is able to mirror the completeness of the whole. No memory stands alone. In Kabbalah, we could say that our Yesod moon shines like a mirror in every world where each part may behold itself in the greater body. And so it is said that within the emanations from Aziluth to Assiah, the worlds are not divided or multiplied, but are a mirror of each other.

Every action leads to a reaction; this is sometimes said to be the law of karma; a consequence coming forth out of movement (action). We must be careful what we generate with our actions, for karma is not simply the reaction to our actions, but the effects that they bring about in the world. In this explanation of karma, our actions can have many different consequences indeed. What is beneficial for one situation could be misfortunate for another. Therefore, what must we do? By conforming with a metaphysical life (law), we start living from principles that are creative and spiritual, instead of living solely from opinions, judgements, and personal preferences.

The mental states that rule the show every day and our intentions, of which we are often not very aware, determine a great deal of our generated karma. We can, by consciousness and free will (soul), not only readjust and alter behavior, but work out karma through spiritual means first. This requires dealing with our thoughts and intentions before they manifest through our body and external, physical life (our personal environment). Redemptive work is part of this, but it also includes prevention of harmful thoughts, feelings, and actions, through insight and foresight.

A question we might wish to ask is: 'What is it that we will to happen?' The 'will' spoken about in this question is the free will. Conscious decisions flow from the soul's vessel of self-consciousness and the seat of conscience. From here, we have access to the subtle ideas and intentions and are able to alter them before they actually manifest through our Assiatic world. In more esoteric terms, we change our actions on the etheric or even astral domain (Yezirah), before they materialise in the physical world of Assiah. Our karma can be a gross or subtle influence in our ability to manifest, meaning that we can think very bad things, but then change their quality and direct them elsewhere within ourselves (diagram I).

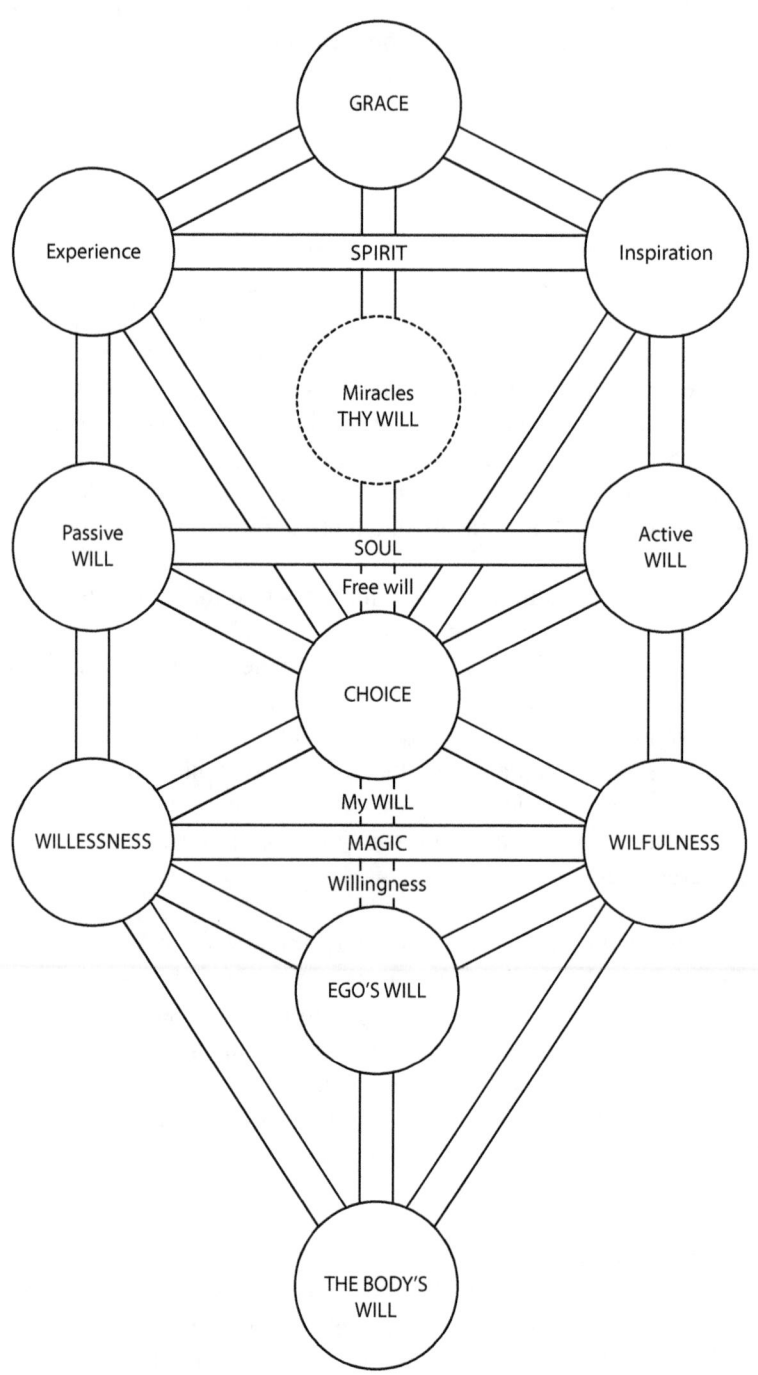

Diagram I

Correction of thought in a spiritual way is done with a subtle and loving attitude towards yourself; guidance of this kind alone will bring the right course of things into being. Punishing or insulting yourself or another backfires on those who claim they have wisdom. Apart from this, it holds great wisdom to know that we have insufficient knowledge to judge over others.

In this stage of our development we are too limited, with some rare exceptions, in our understanding, particularly when you or the other does not know why she or he is punished. So again, let us judge lightly or not at all, but meditate and contemplate diligently.

Our worst self-generated karma and the effects of such actions arise from ignorance and arrogance. This may lead a person or a Kabbalist in particular to the awareness that we cannot live this life by ourselves without the aid of a greater power and intelligence.

In the situation where there is a prolonged effect derived from memory (often through fear and anxiety), emotional processes will generate physical peptides, enzymes, and electrical reactions. Active emotional complexes (triad Chesed-Tifareth-Netzach in Yezirah) will cause chemical-electrical reactions in the corresponding triad in Assiah. Of course, the same goes for the processes at the left side pillar. Individual learned behavior programmes find their way into the central and autonomic nervous system and DNA, where a certain 'software' is installed. Each and every-one of us lives with this kind of mechanism, whether we like it or not. I will say again that such software is vitally necessary. Without it we could not function. What is important in this story about biology and Kabbalah are the personal and negative patterns that sabotage and hinder us in our (spiritual) development.

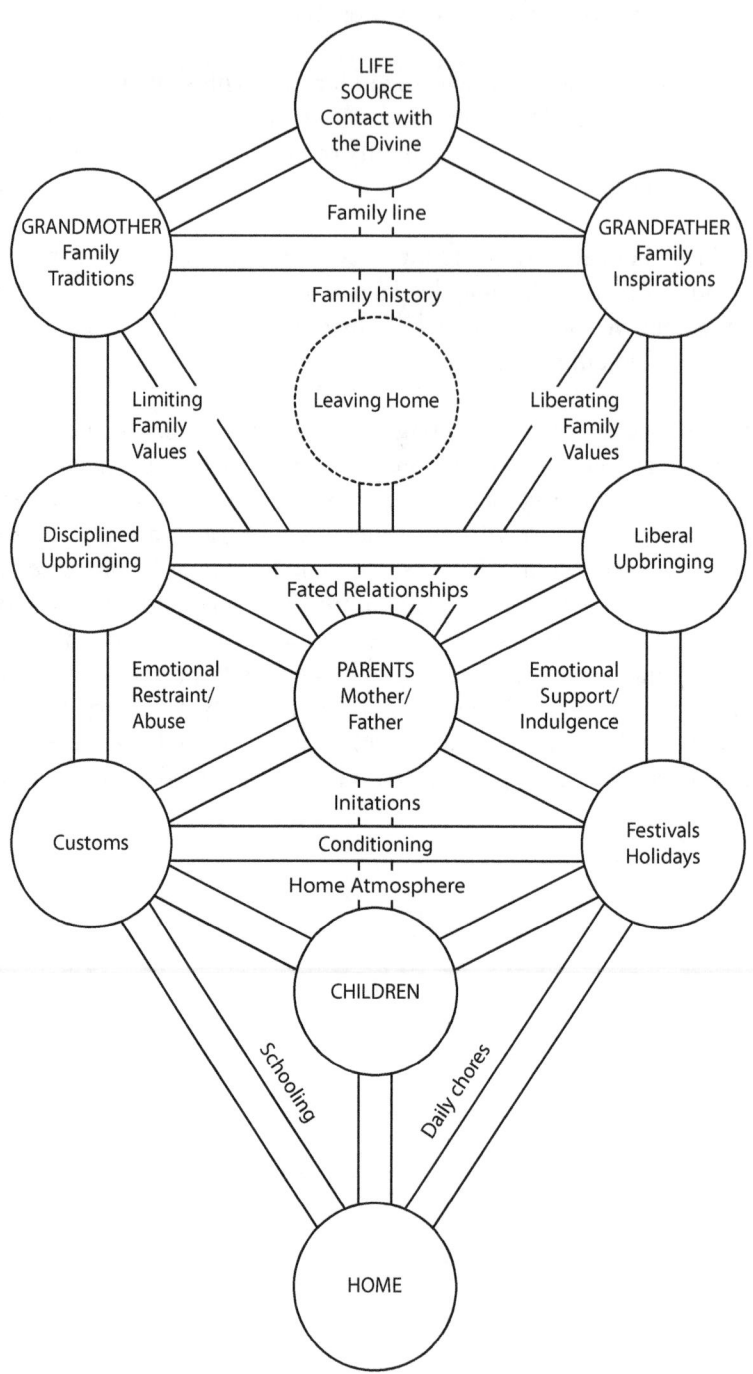

Diagram J

Meditation (Diagram J)

Sit or lie down and come to a state of meditation. Come to a regular rhythm of breathing. Become aware that your memories have fashioned and shaped who you are until this very day. Every thought, emotion, action, and feeling that you carry with you in conscious and unconscious memory are pieces of who you have become today. Our yesterday is the foundation of our present moment. Our present moment is the foundation of our tomorrow. Meditate upon what and who you wish to become. Be aware that the memories we generate at this very moment are who we will be in the next. Use the diagram of the Tree of Life for this particular meditation. See the diagram within you and keep it as a memory of wholeness, harmony, and wisdom. To repeat this memory meditation daily for a few minutes will generate a potent, symbolic memory within you.

Chapter 8: The world of Assiah as a mirror

Our physical body is in a constant mode of flux, mediating between the principles of anabolism and catabolism in that process which we call metabolism. This is a dynamic, alternating exchange between growth and decay which is located at the triad of Tifareth-Gevurah-Chesed of Assiah. The central nervous system, located at the central column at the Tifareth of Assiah, enables the body to regulate itself, tuning as it were into an harmonious movement between the passive and active pillars. From this point of the central nervous system, which is the location of the Malkuth of Yezirah, we enter the first of the lesser halls on Jacob's Ladder, the physical awareness (diagram B). Consciousness of the body has to come from a center, above the rudimentary states and stages of bodily operation that we recognize as mineral, vegetable, and animal (physical). The central nervous system is the first, physical condition from where organic consciousness departs. This implies a type of materialistic causality; as if the physical body is necessary for consciousness to exist. Causality of this kind is sometimes called 'upward causality' in certain scientific circles and the way of evolution or Teshuva in Kabbalah. The opposite of this upward creative causation is a downwards, more religious approach or the way of involution. This can be described as an entanglement of the two reciprocal interdependent processes of involution and evolution. Out of consciousness or Spirit (downwards), physicality enfolds, and out of the formation and making of a physical vehicle, consciousness arises (upwards). One is there within the other (diagram K1 and K2).

It is important that a Kabbalist or a serious student of any esoteric path attends to both the physical body and physical existence. As previously discussed, the world of Assiah is a materialization of all the higher three worlds: Aziluth, Briah, and Yezirah. Assiah is in this respect the fruit of the Tree of Life, and as was once said by a great teacher, '. . . By their fruits you will recognize the Tree ...'

The whole Tree of Life finally presents itself as a physical appearance in a physical world. Although deeper or higher realities are 'hidden' within the density of the physical world, the essence is always there within substantial matter. Our biology is much more than a lump of meat with five senses and is definitely not limited to the physical world. The bottom line here is that the body is a mirror of all the worlds that have descended into Assiah.

Look at your body at this very moment, feel it and sense it. You may watch your breathing for a moment. The state of your body in this moment is exactly how the former worlds have manifested themselves. The body does not lie in that respect. Besides, the physical body is always in the now, whilst the psyche (upper face of Assiah) is moving towards the future and backwards towards the past. At any moment and at any time you can use the body as a mirror for your current state of being.

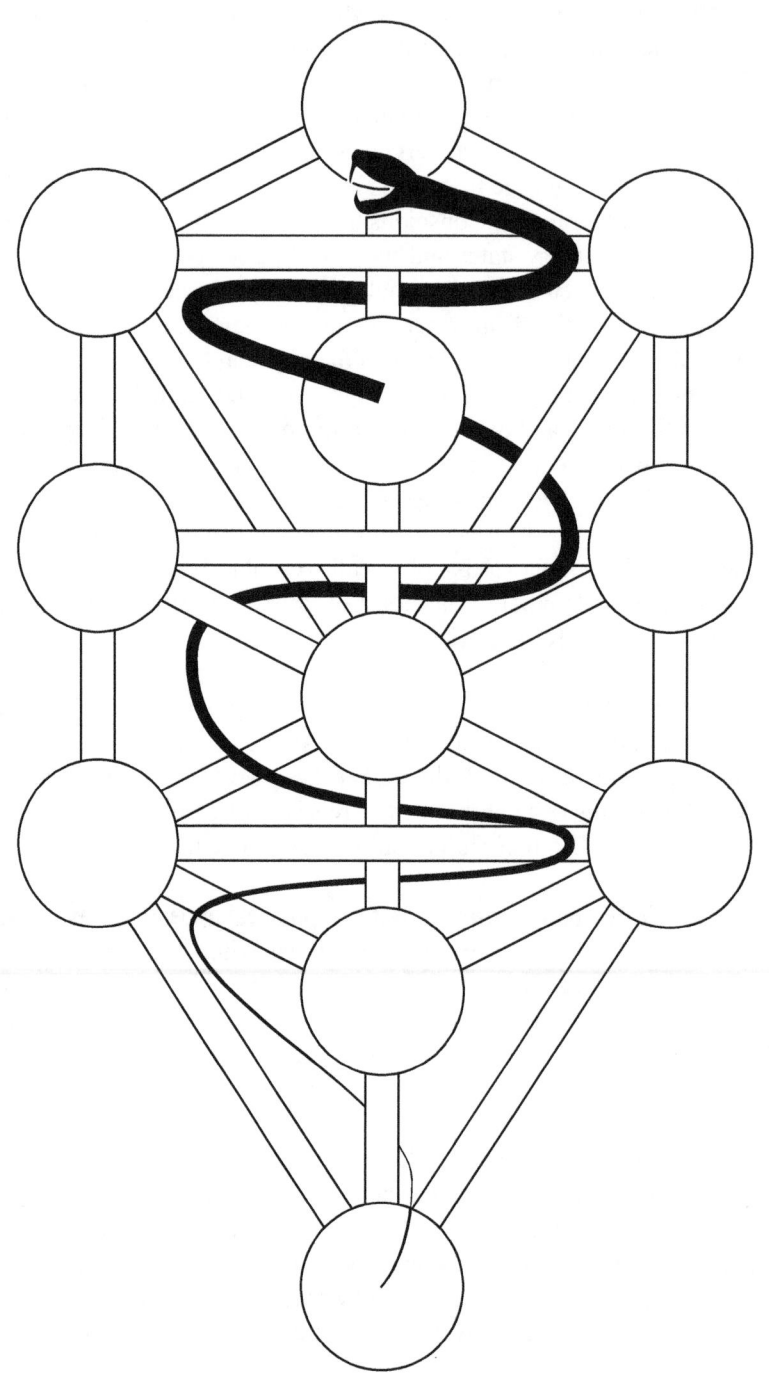

Diagram K1

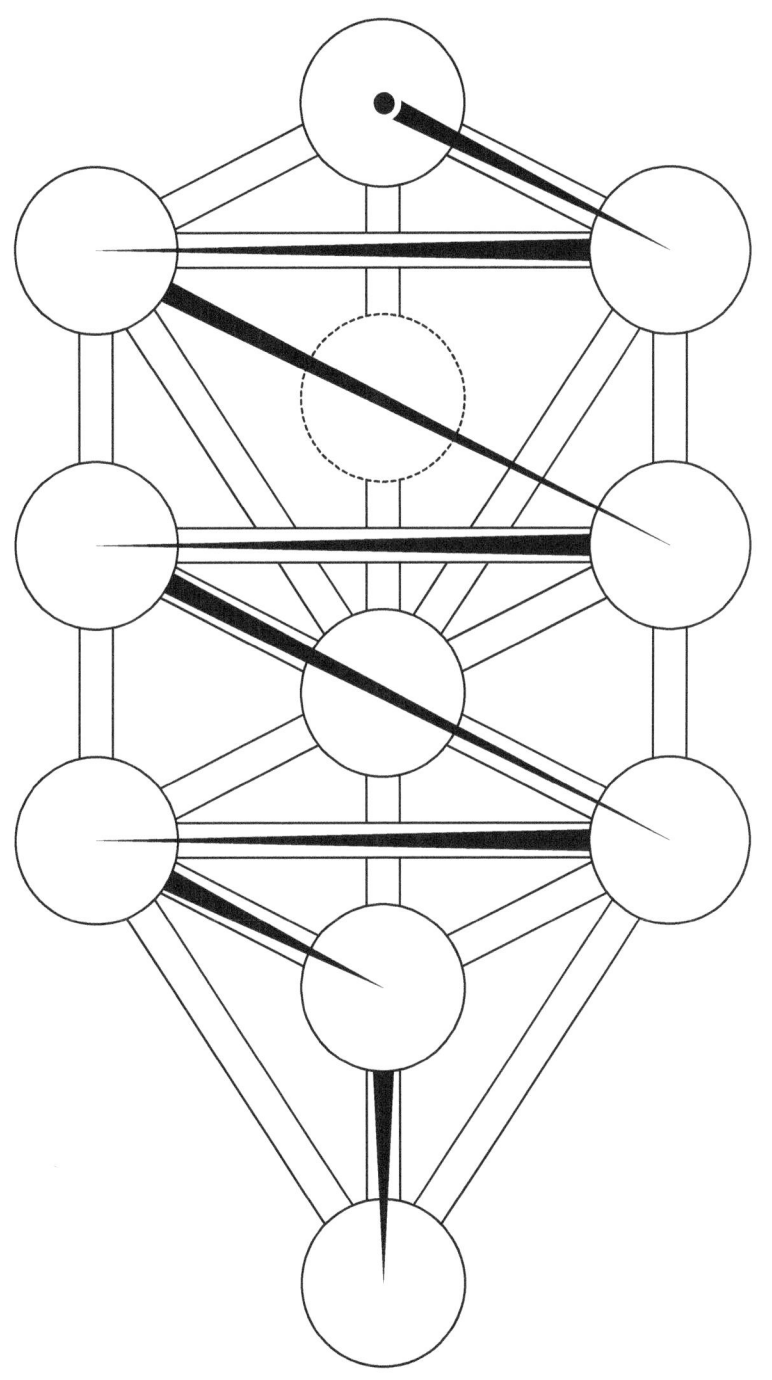

Diagram K2

Meditation

You can do this meditation sitting down or walking. Wherever you are in sitting position or walking, you are in the present moment when you are conscious of the body. Within every breath or movement of the body, you are in the now. Even if your eyes are open and you look at something, be aware that what you see is in the moment of now. If you become aware of the inside of your body, you come to the same experience: what you find here is a result of what was in the past, but you know it only in the present moment. The body is always in the now and never lies. Contemplate this.

From our meditations on the body, we can also distill what data and information are installed and stored in our genes. Particularly when you see old habits of the body and lower psyche which are difficult to break, for they have become fixed patterns within you. Information and data from the psychological and maybe even higher worlds are translated as it were into protein codes (genes).

Genes are minuscule mirrors of what is going on in the greater body. Imagine that the codes of amino acids (proteins) present in the nucleus of the cell are tiny prototypes of information that will determine the codes and structure of the rest of the body. In other words, the structure of genes appears from the inside and the body will be constructed or reconstructed accordingly. Is it a coincidence that genes are a root name for Genesis perhaps? The beginnings of a universe.

The construction of each individual body reflects the structure of the genes contained within it. Every spiritual process and transformation begins with reflection, looking from the inside out and the outside in. To fully understand what is going on in the totality of the body we should detect what information is present within the nucleus and the genes. A principle that brings us back again to the axiom: 'What is above is what is below.'

Hereditary factors are present within us and intermingle with learned and adapted behaviors from our childhood life. For most of us, that is the basis of the physical and lower psychological state of affairs. The mirror of the body therefore shows a clear and accurate representation of our inner landscape. The new biology is called the biology of belief as our belief systems, assumptions, and conditionings, both personal and collective, are the factors which shape the biology of our bodies. How we see ourselves is who we become physically.

This means that with enough perseverance our emotions will manifest into their physical equivalent. A happy and positive person will generate happy-positive hormones, enzymes, proteins, and other chemicals that transform our bodies into that state of emotion. The reverse, as we have seen, is also true and we can 'make and break' ourselves from within.

It is important to remember that this process starts less within the physical vehicle and the DNA-genes, but more on higher levels in the psychological world, where according to a natural hierarchy, our thoughts, emotions, intentions, and perceptions become physically real.

Chapter 9: Perceptions

We stated in chapter 3 that perceptions are simply beliefs in human terms. At the DNA and cellular level, a perception is simply a transmission of information with no personal engagement in it. For a cell to transmit or receive information, the data itself is not interpreted in a personal fashion, but rather it is automatically transferred to the next cell. Perceptions on the macro or human level of the body become beliefs, as they are interpreted by a more subtle psychological level in the upper part of Assiah, centered in Yesod of Yezirah, our personal, daily consciousness.

It is in this center of awareness that information is constantly compared, reflected (memory), analyzed, felt, and evaluated according to our beliefs and previous experiences. Old and new beliefs may be diametrically opposed (rejection) or they may be aligned (acceptance). These are the left and right columns on the Tree of Life respectively.

Ego consciousness is vital for living a life as an individual being. It makes it possible for the psyche to focus on one thing at a time, instead of absorbing and processing all information which comes our way. The Ego-Yesod is the patterning place where we mould and make compositions of our personal experiences.

We cannot do without memory in incarnate life. It is our reference to what we encounter in the present moment, and our tool to anticipate the future. Remember: perception requires memory and memory requires perception. To be an agent of change in your subtle inner life on the level of the psyche (Yezirah) whilst living in the world of the body and genes (Assiah), we need to be people of knowledge through experience.

As is said in Kabbalah, knowledge is power and automatically implies that without knowledge you have little or no power. When we speak of power in Kabbalistic terms, I would like to emphasise the knowledge of oneself, which is true power. Knowledge and power over others has no place in the work of the Kabbalist.

To completely rely on the ideas that our genes control our future will disempower us. These include the ideas that hereditary factors in the genes will control who we become and what will happen to us or that unfortunate diseases that run in the family will come to the surface one day. Such are the beliefs (interpretations) of the information we have received from materialist science over the last decades, e.g., receiving advice from a doctor who tells you that your cholesterol is somewhat high, but you cannot do anything about it, because it is a hereditary problem. With this type of belief and approach to our own bodies (and psyche) we are not only insulting our own intelligence, but the Source-of-all that has provided us with godlike gifts.

Another thing that arises out of this fatalistic belief in genetic fixation is the assumption that there is less or no personal responsibility with regard to one's health. 'I cannot do anything about this . . . I was made this way . . .' are statements given by many people who believe in what they were told or have read, rather than what they have found within themselves.

We know from the Tree of Life that responsibility comes with knowledge and consciousness, which are attributes of the Soul (Tifareth-Gevurah-Chesed of Yezirah).

Being responsible from the soul level means that we 'respond to life' instead of reacting (Yesodic level of belief) and make conscious decisions about what our belief system entails.

I invite you to consider the following: what would happen if I see, hear, and feel my body as a Divine vessel and feel that every particle, from the smallest to the greatest, is a shining, loving, and peaceful unit?

Responsibility is the self-conscious action towards life, beginning with your own inner landscape and all the actions that contain it concerning the world of Assiah, which includes our personal world.

Finding excuses for our state of being and health is not always valid anymore. Of course, although we are talking about a theory that can be applied on a daily basis, there are still problems that we cannot change at the present moment. This does not alter the current theory but says more about human possibilities and how to apply this theory in practical terms.

Another belief that we have adopted from science is the assumption that the genes have the same function in the cell as the brain has in the body. It is comparable to the central control tower of all the vital functions in the body. Like in an airport, the control tower is of the greatest importance, making sure all traffic (information) will 'land and depart' efficiently and safely. This control center, providing and regulating, balancing and harmonizing, is the Tifareth of Assiah.

To change this perception is not so difficult and can happen in an instant. Beliefs are related to how we feel about things being a personal experience through our thoughts and actions or passive and active bio-psychological processes (triad Yesod-Hod-Netzach of Yezirah).

These beliefs and feelings have their corresponding place in the body where the visceral organs are located, giving us the so called 'gut feeling'. Our psyche and body may communicate certain beliefs simultaneously in the psyche in the form of feelings and bodily sensations. These feelings and beliefs have an intelligence of their own, and should not be seen as inferior expressions of the natural human being. The problem that may and does arise out of ignorance and superstition is a belief that was born out of the wrong motivations, such as fear, anxiety, anger, or low self-esteem.

Perceptions do not only come from a sense of sight, but from all senses, together with thought, feelings, and actions. A perception is always subjective, and thus our belief is also subjective. We may believe in the same thing, but the way we believe is always different from the other person's way. The world we perceive is a phenomenon that is always connected with how we experience the world about us. The cell operates from these subjective perceptions between itself and the environment. But there is more. The way we think and feel about our own body is communicated through chemical and electrical means, in the endocrine and nervous systems respectively. These chemical and electrical signals find their way towards the cell and the genes within it.

Perception that comes from the macrocosm of the natural organism (Tree of Assiah) shapes and gives form to (but does not determine) the internal chemistry and perception of the microcosm of the cell. We see a hierarchy here once more that shows that the events which play out in the macrocosm do affect and influence the microcosm. Perception comes from the three lower worlds on Jacob's Ladder, as the worldly and the cosmic are not separate but rather integrated. Human beings have the potential to perceive the world and themselves in the whole scope of the three worlds (diagram A and B).

On the middle pillar the Sefirot explain the way we are able to perceive in different worlds and with different 'eyes'. Malkuth perceives the physical dimension, putting together the elementary world that the senses can comprehend. The body or vehicle of Malkuth is tailored to live in this physical-biological environment. Moreover, the physical body comes forth out of the earth (womb), having been 'called forth, created, formed, and made' to walk on the earth.

The so-called 'fall from Eden' was a cosmic consequence of free will, so that the psyche could manifest in the tenth emanation. Yesod has the ability to form a personal relationship with the world, being able to perceive the personal world inside, related to the direct (personal) environment. Besides, from our psychological Yesod, we can be aware of the body and the interaction between the body and psyche.

Tifareth plays a very different role in this respect, in that it represents the self (psyche), perceiving the 'outside' (Malkuth, Yesod) and the mineral, vegetable, and animal level of the natural Tree, and the inside or spiritual Briatic life. Tifareth is located in the psyche and consciousness where Solomon has its seat (throne), and the three lower worlds meet (diagram A and B).

Malkuth is only inclusive to itself, while Yesod can include the body in addition to itself (lower psyche or personal domain). Tifareth is able to encompass both of these aforementioned levels, perceiving from a 'silent witness' position. Here we become aware of being aware, while we engage and include the levels below and above. These processes come together in what we call the soul. The soul has its own perception of reality, being the vehicle of consciousness, and is our spiritual compass which endeavors to work towards unity and wholeness.

You can imagine that the more we live and have our being from this perception of Tifareth and the Soul, letting them be, as it were, the captain of our ship, we would 'sail' a different kind of life.

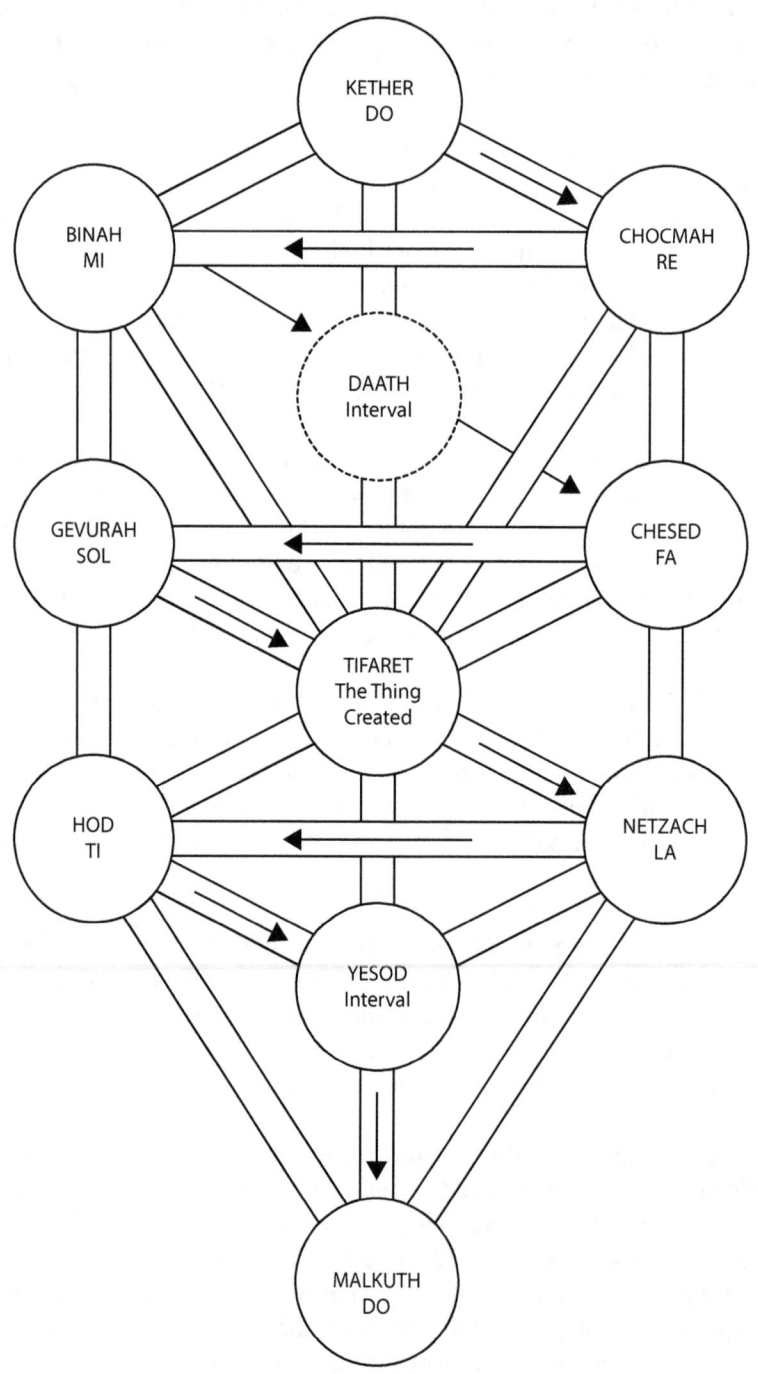

Diagram L

What story would we tell to our lower personal psyche and our body? What inner consequences would this have for our natural life? The Soul and Tifareth could attune to the higher worlds, making the natural vehicle (Tree of Assiah) a vessel for the higher worlds to flow down into.

In the preparation towards this end, the Kabbalist works on the process of purifying her/himself, in order that the influence of the higher worlds may be not only received, but also sustained and understood. It is a matter for the laws of octaves and frequencies (diagram L) to determine to what degree we prepare the natural world of Assiah for reception. After all, that is the meaning of Kabbalah, to receive. Another expression for receiving is making oneself available for the higher worlds. The more we are able to do this, the more reliable we are for the Source, and able to work in harmony with providence.

Meditation

This meditation brings us once more to the Tree of Life. Imagine and feel it's image within you. Kether as a crown on the head, Chocmah and Binah on either side of the head. Daath around the head and throat, Chesed and Gevurah at the right and left shoulders, Tifareth at the heart center/breastbone, Netzach and Hod at the right and left hips, Yesod at the pelvis and genitals, and Malkuth between the feet. You may do this meditation standing or sitting or even walking if you have practiced enough to do so. Connect the 22 paths between the Sefirot. Do not place any names or images in your inner Tree. Merely keep your Tree empty like an open vessel. Now make an intention to be available to the Source of all, to Divinity and the cosmos. Be open. Expect nothing, expect everything.

Chapter 10: Changes and consequences

All this work will change our inner biology, attuning, responding, and living our incarnate life along universal laws, particularly the laws that govern and move the lower worlds towards all metaphysical qualities and values including harmony, balance, compassion, and love. The Kabbalist does nothing by chance or accident, but consciously works and takes action towards these inner structures. Even more so, the Kabbalist does not stop at a belief system, but is interested in Truth (Tifareth) and true Knowledge (Daath).

The work of the Kabbalist will change the physiology of the body, influencing the core and nucleus of each cell. As such, the Kabbalist becomes literally and physically the Knowledge that she/he receives. This is what we mean in esoteric terms when we say that we 'embody' something. Thus, we are able to embody knowledge and higher virtues.

We form the appropriate subtle vehicles of thoughts, feelings, ideas and memories through the Yeziratic world, moulding our inner Tree of Life. These metaphysical influences finally become matter in and throughout our physical body (Malkuth). This is what we literally call to bring heaven to earth in Kabbalah, which in this explanation is much more than a metaphor.

Out of consciousness we shape our vehicle, and through that vehicle, we become consciousness.

This is a saying of an intrinsic entanglement that explains the co-dependency, or rather the interdependency between consciousness and matter.

Co-dependent life is more than cooperation, but becomes in unity with the experience of self (psychological self in the world of Yezirah). The human body consists of many different cells, tissues, organs, and organ systems, making the total organism or the biological self. Do the parts know that they are separate? It has been proven that they all have a sense of Self but they cannot regard themselves as an 'I' outside of the totality of the other organs.

Competition in this sense leads to tension that invites life to discover each other. That is, it does not compete in ways that destroy the others through overbearing expansion. Cooperation should be challenged by competition and tension in order that the functions and purposes of the unit are being tested and brought under conscious consideration.

These are the dynamics between the archetypal forces of the side pillars on the Tree and in nature—Chesed and Gevurah or Jupiter and Mars. They should be constantly observed, checked, and corrected by a monitor. This monitor is the solar archetype (Tifareth) that expresses self (consciousness), awareness of context, and harmony and has a gathering or unifying intelligence. The solar intelligence in nature is equivalent to the solar consciousness within the human body, the subtle body system (chakra) and the spiritual energy of Self.

The message of many great teachers has always included the quality of Tifareth—unifying, cooperation, integration, inclusiveness. In other words, love.

Evolution in the biochemical sense appears to travel in a horizontal direction as many species of all kinds exchange information not only via sensory means, but literally through exchange of DNA (genes). The simplest example is through procreation, yet there are other, more profound examples of exchange. In the spiritual respect, we must also look for more horizontal ways for evolutionary exchange, not simply to build towers or ladders to 'climb to heaven' but to regard and behold the 'next step' in the horizontal domain. In Kabbalah, this would mean that our spiritual life is expressed through our daily thoughts, feelings, and actions (the greater vegetable triad). Spiritual development happens not only through the vertical axis or middle pillar, but by means of integrating the vertical and horizontal. While the horizontal life is more occupied with the personal, the vertical relates to consciousness and the transpersonal. As long as we are living a life from the perception of our ego (my, mine, and me), we will not develop very much or at all. Interesting in all of this is the effort some scientists have undertaken to find the so called 'selfish gene'. This gene displays the behavior of out-competing others in order to survive and become better in the chain of evolution. The idea of being bad, of prestige, attainment, etc., goes hand-in-hand with this selfish gene. Not being good enough is the emotional-psychological and social input to 'move' people and to constantly attain a level of higher enlightenment and take more out of life. Again this is a mechanistic and horizontal, linear-time-related view.

Nature is hard and tough, and the only way to make it liveable is to rise above it, to conquer it. A world of struggle and war of 'good versus evil' instead of love, trust, compassion, and the practical side of those qualities, such as cooperation, empathy, support, and collective effort. That is at least the opinion of certain neo-Darwinists.

Human culture has the adaptability to shift from a genetic fact towards conscious decision making. Genetic fact means the way we have looked at genes as a fixed biological programme within the physical body. This new way of looking at genes is a new way of engineering our own biology. Our involvement and exchange with the environment is of crucial importance for making changes in our biology. This can easily lead, as it often does, towards opportunistic ways of making nature serve human needs, instead of living in accordance with nature. The Kabbalist works towards unity and thereby to a homeostasis or harmony in the physical world.

Is it the gene that is the headmaster of the organism? Does the change in the cell come from the gene, depending on how the chromosomes are organized and regulating the organism? Or is the interaction between organism and organic world the most important factor which moves the interior and exterior?

Let's look at some significant facts that speak in favour of our current Kabbalistic-Scientific endeavour:

1. Replication of cells can only take place with multiple stimuli from the environment and through the help of different genes (not just one); cooperation is needed.
2. DNA produces RNA. This indicates that DNA is a reproductive organ and does not function like a brain.
3. Competition is the first step in evolution to come to the conclusion that an opponent is a cooperative partner and not the enemy.
4. Cooperation is not synonymous with building or expansion, but thrives on the mutual agreement that a homeostasis should be between building (expansion) and breaking down (contraction).
5. To solely expand is to eventually conquer, which leads to the disease of the organism and/or psyche.
6. However, conquering in nature can be done in two ways:
    1. By power and use of manipulation, i.e., overthrowing leaders, forcing the submission and the slavery of others (see point 5) and
    2. By love and compassion, i.e., integrating, sharing, and including.

Chapter 11: Kabbalah in practice

We have read about some of the implications that the new biology talks about in the six points above when it comes to influencing genes through conscious participation in life. These points invite us to work actively (right side column) with the new theory (left side column) and integrate these ideas in a way that complements the work of unification. This is the work of the Kabbalist.

The importance of cooperation
Let us examine the first point above, which explains that cooperation is needed to facilitate true change (transformation). This means that for a Kabbalist to move from the active sphere into the sphere of growth and into the upper sphere of transformation, we must bring all the different parts of ourselves (our Tree of Life) and all these circles in the Tree of Life (diagram G) into a cooperative whole. These circles encompass the Tree from a lower level or sphere (Yesod at the center) to a middle circle (Tifareth at the center) and an upper circle or sphere (with Daath at the center). There is no exclusion here, for excluding a part of the whole is to obstruct cooperation. All Sefirot and paths should be included in this work.

Now we have an additional piece of essential information in our hands. For the more we integrate the whole Tree within, the more we influence the immediate structure of the cell: the DNA and genes.

Replication of cells does not mean unlimited growth without guidance and limitation towards that growth, i.e., unlimited Chesed (expansion) without the controlling force of Gevurah (contraction). Replication means a regeneration (Yesod) of cells, coming from a systematic and organized intelligence (Tifareth). In such an intelligent organization, each part of the system has its place and is recognized as a vital link in the total chain, complementing the function of the total being (organism). Likewise, it was said in the classical works of Kabbalah that the Tree is only complete within the number Ten. There are ten digits, ten circles, ten Sefirot, ten expressions or names of God. Not eleven and not nine.

It is the typical consciousness and intelligence of Tifareth to move towards cooperation, as it, like the sun, is an intelligence of gathering and integrative cooperation. In the Sepher Yezirah (Book of Formation), Tifareth is named the mediating and also the collective intelligence, as it gathers and organizes the conditions for harmony and balance in and around itself. Each cell has a nucleus around which electrons circle, imitating as it were a mini-solar system. That same nucleus is a mediating or collecting intelligence, gathering, forming, and keeping objects in harmony around itself. Whatever happens within our psychological Tifareth, or preferably higher in the Briatic world where the Shekinah rests in Tifareth, happens within the Tifareth of the physiological body. Harmony, balance, and truth will be a part of our biological life within atoms, molecules, cells, tissues, organs, and the entire body.

To begin seeing yourself as a whole being, like a universe that organises and harmonises itself, is the start of cooperation and replication (rejuvenation). The organising spiritual essence behind all of this is the Shekinah—the Holy Presence within the Kingdom of Aziluth and therefore within the Malkuth of every subsequent world. The Shekinah can be found (as She is in Exile in matter) in the Malkuth of Malkuth. This is the Kingdom of Kingdoms, the spiritual core where all the descending worlds (Briah, Yezirah, Assiah) have been created, formed, and made.

All existent expressions of life in the Malkuth of Assiah testify of the Shekinah presence through their own being and living/existence. To move into matter is likewise approaching the Shekinah, liberating Her from the bondage of exile. Simultaneously, the Shekinah sets the human soul free from its inherent ignorance obtained by coming into the material world.

That means the Kabbalist in his or her work unravels the different layers or worlds (garments) that are present and surround the Divine center which lies at the heart of everything. Each part is necessary for the whole, and the whole is greater than the sum of its parts. Implicit in the living center at the heart of all Assiatic expression in Malkuth, the Shekinah is like the Divine DNA that holds all that was, is, and shall ever be (diagram A).

A timeless center that is within time-space, the foundation (at the heart, Tifareth) of Creation, the Shekinah remains the spiritual core, wherefrom the worlds unfold from moment to moment. In tradition, although the Shekinah can be sought after, She will only reveal herself when the right time is there to receive Her.

Exercise
Be aware in your daily actions, thoughts, and feelings that all you do, think, and feel is an expression of the Shekinah. Your first breath when waking up is the breath of the Shekinah. Your first thought is that of the Shekinah, and the first thing that you feel is of the Shekinah. As you continue your day with breathing, acting, thinking, and feeling, be aware of your experience of the Shekinah in all these expressions.

Be available to Her, as she is present in every single moment of your life, day and night. Let your actions, your customs, and routines become a dedication to the Shekinah. Feel how all life orchestrates around the Shekinah as She leads all to cooperation, complementation, and harmony.

Let your life be in service of Her, knowing that this life is not yours, but has been given to you in order to return it to the Shekinah.

DNA is a reproductive organ not a brain
To elucidate our second point, it is worth introducing another Kabbalistic vision, derived from the scriptures of Genesis. As DNA generates RNA in its own likeness, so it is said in Genesis that 'God (Elohim) created them in its own image and likeness'. I would like to add, referring to the first book of Genesis, where God the immovable creates 'other' in its likeness. Here we come to an old Kabbalistic mystery, the origin of which lies within many traditions, proclaiming that Kether is Malkuth and Malkuth is Kether. In Kabbalah it is said that Kether is the essence, while Malkuth is the substance (of the same thing).

Be that as it may, we can find an analogy here with the DNA and RNA. DNA contains all information, but is itself confined within each particular cell. Like Kether, it needs to mirror itself into another object to make itself known. This object is a created reflection of the original that is expressed in time and space. RNA is this movable reflection of DNA, functioning in the world of action, moving forward and sending out information that is contained in the fixed and unmovable center of its own circle.

Kether by itself is not creative but 'calls forth' or is the 'Word' that utters itself, naming Who-He Is, whereby a second and a third come into creative life (Chocmah and Binah). The creative parents come out of this utterance. In analogy, DNA calls forth that which is held in its 'point' or nucleus out of its own being. RNA is the forthcoming movement of Wisdom and Understanding. DNA in the body is normally regarded as material substance, but as it is a construction of information, it may also be regarded as a mental or even a spiritual substance.

Competitive opponent or cooperative partner?
The third point directly follows on from the second. Competition is not something that should not be. Competition is a necessary part of existence. Competition occurs in nature all the time, from the cosmic scale to the minuscule. Competition is where the tension increases between the left and right pillars on the Tree of Life and becomes less complementary. If competition has a purpose, it would be to find a complementary and cooperative fusion between one extreme and the other. Tension in nature is natural, but it is not a goal in itself; in fact, what would be the point? Tension, attraction, and repulsion are forces between the opposites in the cosmos that eventually (always) move towards balance and harmony (Tifareth position on the Tree of Life).

The longer in time and farther in space the opposites (pillars) are placed relative to one another, the more we suffer their consequences. In daily terms, this manifests as war, fighting, conflict, and tension, but it also contains symptoms like sickness, fatigue, psychosomatic illness, high blood pressure, and heart failure. These examples demonstrate how nature compensates when the positions of the pillars remain apart, rather than coming together towards cooperation.

Unfortunately, the human being has the capacity to move against the natural cause of things and against the law of harmony that brings opposites into union. Although no being can ever obstruct or corrupt Cosmic and Divine Law, we can sabotage our own life by not moving in accordance with these natural laws.

In order to cooperate, we need wisdom, understanding, and Knowledge (Daath) of ourselves, the other, the world, and how Divinity plays a part in this whole scheme. A dilemma is generated from ignorance of ourselves in the first instance, followed automatically by ignorance of others, the world, and finally of God.

Cooperation can only succeed if Knowledge (Daath) of Self (Tifareth) is present in the process while the view of ourselves, the world, and the cosmos slowly extends beyond the limited boundaries of our worldly perspective. Any creatures or species that work together, including cells, require self-knowledge in relation to their environment in order to make cooperative connections and begin working towards inclusivity and union. This is clearly the work of the Kabbalist and the work of nature. We can conclude from this that the Kabbalist does indeed work in accordance with nature.

Cooperation thrives on equilibrium between expansion and contraction

Cooperation is not synonymous with building or expansion, but thrives on the mutual agreement that a homeostasis is maintained between building (expansion) and breaking down (contraction).

In the fourth point, we see the appearance of the principles of cosmic expansion (Chesed) and contraction (Gevurah). These are the right and left pillars respectively. In many examples within Kabbalah, questions arise about this relationship between Chesed and Gevurah and the right and left pillars. Often, Gevurah is regarded as 'evil', as opposed to Chesed being 'good'. On the level of and in the world of metaphysical principles (Briah), there is no sense of 'right and wrong'. Briah is the world of essential principles, explaining how things work in the universe. That is why they are called metaphysical or creative principles.

To use terms like 'right and wrong' is an attempt to qualify the creative principles of expansion and contraction, sometimes called 'construction and destruction'. However applicable to moral-human life, these principles are translations that explain relative-cultural interpretations of what expansion and contraction mean. As we become conscious of the principles of Chesed and Gevurah in human life, we begin to see their relative meanings in how we interpret them (diagram E).

Then we see through the cultural, religious, political, and economic constructions in time and space. Natural life, like the human body, does not interpret these principles, but 'lives them'. We build different perspectives of the creative (Briatic) principles from the human psyche. What they become is a set of ethical rules, religious dogma, law, etc. As long as a natural balance is inherent and maintained within our interpretations, we respect the natural way of the universe. Unfortunately, this is not always the case, as we can see in the example of how we look at 'economy' from a human perspective, in comparison to the natural economy. Nature keeps a constant balance and rebalance in its flow between expansion and contraction which is easily seen in the four seasons.

Often, we do not listen to how our own body turns in accordance with the wheel of nature, thus going against nature by accumulation and consumerism (expansion). This is just one example, but look beyond our physical body, and see how the 'economy' is played out.

The stock exchange is 'not well' if there is no growth (expansion) but rather is seen as a decline in statistics (contraction). The general approach appears to be that the economy should grow in order to be 'good'. However, without the compensation of contraction, the uncontrolled growth thus goes against natural order.

Expanding into disease
To expand is to eventually conquer and leads to the disease of the organism and/or psyche.

In the fifth point, which extends upon the fourth one, self-consciousness makes the human being realise that tribal awareness is not bringing us any further than the vegetable and animal levels of nature. Tribalism includes some cooperation and inclusivity, but only within the boundaries that conform with the limits of the tribe-consciousness of the group. This cooperation does not go further than our family, cultural, and/or religious group. There remains a sense of 'us' against 'others' that are also confined to tribal boundaries, seeing often the differences against their own identity.

Moreover, cooperation of this kind is based on ideologies that enforce this self-generated identity. The more we identify with a group, the more we become separate from others who think that they are right in their ideas and identity. Around the larger triad Hod-Netzach-Malkuth, with Yesod in Yezirah at the center, we find the tribal-vegetable nature. Cooperation, interaction, socializing needs, and affection have all their place between people here.

However, the personal engagement with external life (society) is based upon what is accepted and what is not (reward and punishment). Even within tribal communities, we find different sub-cultures, but they are always limited by what they regard as their tribal truth, or what they see in the psychological mirror of Yesod.

Our ego constructs 'truth' from what it has learned and copies behavior from deep collective, psychological, and biological influences. To these heights, our tribal consciousness and the ego living within it, cooperation is a possibility. Beyond the horizon of this consciousness, lies the 'enemy' of the others (unbelievers), who cannot cooperate in the eyes of the tribe. Of course, all tribes say the same thing, as they base their so-called truth upon subjective, relative, and transient experience (diagrams G and J).

Looking at the Tree of Life and specifically at Jacob's Ladder, we see immediately that only a part of the whole (like one-fifth) is known in the vegetable triad. The natural Tree or world of Assiah is viewed here, with perhaps some contact with the Self at the Tifareth of Yezirah and therefore, pre-awakening states in the animal triad. The dependency on the community, society, and ethics is very strong, leaving many egos bound to the group vessel, with limited cooperation with their own group members.

When we recognize the archetypes as psycho-spiritual parts of ourselves, and not only as external, mythical fantasy beings, we begin the process of integration, inclusivity, and cooperation.

The myths of the classical world were not written by primitives, but were, and still are, cosmic tales, describing the principles inherent in the universe generally, and in human life specifically.

Mythical stories that are known all over the world in many times and places are showing us the interactions between the different archetypes, acting out a cosmic play which we can recognize within the world of the psyche. As was said: 'The wars in heaven are the wars in our soul'.

What does it take for both a human individual and every cell in our body to cooperate within the whole? We need to shift level, from a tribal-personal perspective firstly towards a world-centered perspective (Tifareth) and then beyond, into the cosmic, transpersonal world of Briah.

The creative and metaphysical world of Briah is about inclusivity, which leads naturally to cooperation. Cosmic Law reflects natural order, and although there is still polarity and duality at play, the forces that work here (archangels) direct and orchestrate all things towards harmonious cooperation.

Once connected to the forms (left pillar) and forces (right pillar) of Briah, we align with the archetypes that represent this creative domain. Through working our way 'up' into the world of creativity, we consciously encounter the different archetypes, who are sentinels and messengers of the different spiritual qualities in the macrocosm and microcosm alike.

When we recognize the archetypes as psycho-spiritual parts of ourselves, and not only as external, mythical fantasy beings, we begin the process of integration, inclusivity, and cooperation. The myths of the classical world were not written by primitive minds, but were, and are still, cosmic scenarios, describing the principles inherent in the universe generally, and in human life specifically.

Allegorically, the fight between archangels and demons is a deep, unconscious battle within the human mind. A release of tension, frustration, anger, and other emotions is at the base of these mythic battles, for it is exactly these emotions that the corresponding archetypes represent (diagram F).

Ways of conquering
However, conquering in nature can be done in two ways:
- By power and use of manipulation, i.e., overthrowing leaders, forcing the submission and the slavery of others, and
- By love and compassion, i.e., integrating, sharing, and including.

Point six refers to the innate impulse in nature to dominate by force, or by the law of the jungle. In animals, territory is as important as a house or shelter is for a human being. It provides safety and security, facilitating the right conditions for the species to be contained and flower. The human-animal nature is no exception to this behavior, struggling and competing to have their piece of earth somewhere.

In times when survival is needed, there is strife and the necessity to obtain these conditions, but even within the established societies of today (and the past), we compete endlessly beyond our necessities to have what others possess. Survival of the fittest. A law of tooth and claw.

Conquering and domination are the natural expression of the animal instincts that we all possess.

The difference with the external natural world, where expansion stops and ceases when there is enough to provide the security and food, is when our human-animal moves beyond necessities, into what it 'wants'. Fortunately, domination occurs not only through conquering by force, but also through love and compassion. Here, free will is always given first to our fellow creatures. By giving love, care, compassion, harmony, we provide the other with the conditions to choose.

Exercise
Take a moment to sit still with eyes open or closed. Observe and be conscious of what happens to you sitting still whilst not moving physically. Now, take your psychological attention away from your external life by drawing in thoughts and feelings. Those thoughts you recognize as memories (past) and those that involve the future.

In a subtle way, try to be still in yourself. Pay no attention to your surroundings. You will notice that there are impulses coming from the body and psyche that have a tendency to draw you away from stillness. A restless animal-human nature distracts you and invites you to move, activate, and initiate. Try to remain in your position of stillness and do not get angry or agitated at yourself. Merely guide the inner animal as if it were your pet animal who needs some discipline and love.

Chapter 12: Programmed for life

We are psychologically and biologically programmed from birth to learn from the world as though in a hypnotic state. Children's brains work under the influence of a theta brainwave state up to the age of eight years. That state of awareness is similar to hypnosis, to the imaginative mind and the power of suggestion. Those theta brainwaves are extremely sensitive and receptive to the impulses that come from the outside world. The child absorbs and incorporates the information that is learned from and taught by the external world. In fact, the child learns to become what she/he has been given from the outside in.

This way of learning is unconscious for the most part, serving our human world by following the programmes that our parents taught us. Almost similar to downloading a piece of software, the child is instructed through the senses, the tools of the physical body, to copy the programmes of the parents. There is very little consciousness involved in this process, and nature does not expect it to be conscious either.

Living the programme is the same as living in a cycle of behavior that does not ask for conscious involvement. Consciousness is the creative part of ourselves. If that awakens within us, we start to become conscious of the programmeming. Before this, we do not even know that we are living a programme. To move out of such a programme is to become aware of where we find obstructions in our life. This shows us that we are struggling and cannot move further. Often these are not signs that show us that we should stop moving in a particular direction. Rather, it means the opposite, that we find a dimension of our life that we have not met before and hence, a part of our life that does not match with our programme. It is said in many wisdom traditions: 'Where you struggle is where your growth is'.

When you are on a smooth path with no trouble or challenges, you will inevitably continue on the programmed path generated by your upbringing. To bring your life from the deep unconscious programming to the subconscious levels where new learning is possible, it is helpful to use suggestion and repetition. Suggestive learning is a way of symbolically giving your subconscious different input. These symbols should be chosen consciously and related to what new psychological pattern we would like to integrate. By repetition, the subconscious starts to gradually integrate these symbols and accepts them as a new part of the inner structure of the human psyche. The Kabbalist uses the suggestions of the Tree of Life and the corresponding symbols therein.

In order to learn spiritually, we need to rise above our own conditionings or programmes. The Kabbalist should rise at least into the human-animal level, where there is an experience of pre-awakening. This mode of consciousness has no creativity yet and can, like an animal, learn by repetition and suggestion. Although from the human-animal level we are able to move our life out of our personal programme, we do not completely escape the conditionings and emotional dependency that are present in the programme.

To rewrite our programme, we need to become 'like little children' as Jesus Christ said when he told his people what they should do to enter the Kingdom of Heaven.

We have to start living a life of wonder again and go back into that innocent state where we are completely open to suggestions. Making a new programme means that we are living that new programme. The Kingdom of Heaven is the Tifareth of Yezirah at the Malkuth of Briah. Our thoughts, feelings, and actions should be in alignment and in accord with the new life and programme that we brought forth.

These are the psychological triads in the lower face of the Tree of Yezirah. The ego is the focal point where first of all, old learning has taken root, and where we make changes in our personal programming. Although the physical body, the lower face of Assiah, will follow the new programme when all the psychological parts are working as one, it is very helpful if we instruct our physical body and behavior as well. For example, when we rewrite our psychological and biological programming to get rid of destructive thoughts, we should stop self-sabotaging and hitting ourselves and calling ourselves bad names.

Escaping the programme is done by working through the cycles of our own psyche. The incorporation of a new programme leads to changes in behaviour and often to changes in consciousness. However, it does not necessarily lead to a transformation of consciousness, where old patterns are completely taken apart and put together into a new form.

In other words, we can learn or unlearn through the power of the psyche and the suggestive unconscious mind. This can transform our being through the higher psychological domain (Yezirah) through use of the archetypal world of Briah and the consciousness of self in the Tifareth of Yezirah. Those of us who are in contact with the Holy Spirit are those who can make changes at will. These are always changes that have transcended the necessities of the personality. If we do not alter our conditionings and routines in any way, we give up our free will to the will of the programme.

Leading such a life is living someone else's life. Following such path is following someone else's path.

Kabbalah is the work of unity and means not only to raise human consciousness to a transcendent level, but to integrate all levels into one consciousness. Kabbalah is an inclusive mystical path where life is an integral part of the inner work. Routines or programmes are not wrong, we can simply not live without them as they move many vital processes of our physical and psychological being unconsciously.

Within this work of unification, the Kabbalist regulates life along the lines of self-made routines that contain symbolic and mystical expressions of one's own life. Therefore, many routines do not need to disappear or change as they can be reinterpreted from a deeper level of experience.

The Kabbalist may transform a simple dinner into a holy act or walk the street contemplating the Presence of God in all he or she meets. There is no opportunity that cannot be changed into a Kabbalistic exercise. Again, this does not mean we have to change our whole personality, but guide our thinking, feeling, and doing into mystical experiences.

This connects to the biological paradigm, stating that we do change our biology to the very nucleus and DNA of the cell by making changes in consciousness.

Personal programs and routines that make us anxious, afraid, sad, or angry or that initiate any other negative experience can be changed and even transformed.

It is good to remember that our everyday personal self or ego cannot initiate these changes but functions like a perfect mirror, reflecting what is already within our psychological programme. Only consciousness from the psychological self or Tifareth is able to be creative, creating ourselves again in an image that we choose freely and consciously.

PART 2 - Introduction: Quantum Physics

What is quantum physics? There is not one definition of this scientific discipline, although most scientists agree about one thing: it is a weird science that can almost not be understood by the intellect. It was said by Niels Bohr, 'If you think you have understood quantum physics you have not understood it'.

Quantum physics developed over many decades, formulated as a set of controversial mathematical explanations or experiments that classical physics could not explain. These equations were sometimes called speculative, for they measured probabilities, rather than objective outcomes. It began at the turn of the twentieth century, around the same time that Albert Einstein published his theory of relativity, a separate mathematical revolution in physics that describes the motion of things at high speeds. Unlike relativity, however, the origins of quantum physics cannot be attributed to any one scientist. Rather, multiple scientists contributed to a foundation of these principles.

For example, consider the discovery and behaviour of particles of light. Light can appear both as waves and as particles. The discovery meant that something (like a photon or light particle) could have different properties and therefore appear in more than one way. That matter can behave like a wave (energy) and like a particle (solid), dependent on the observer effect of who was looking, is maybe the greatest mystery of all. Quantum science is exploring the micro or subatomic world of infinite possibilities, endless space and information. The paradox that we find in this subatomic world explains how a whole new universe can exist in tiny little spaces with energy and intelligence far beyond what we can imagine. Consciousness is a major component in quantum theory, for it is from consciousness that matter becomes something. The way that consciousness observes the world is the way that matter (subatomic particles) responds. Consciousness gives rise and shape to the material world (diagram M).

The Kabbalah understands that everything is interactively connected, which is explained through cosmology and the Tree of Life. Besides, it teaches that creation exists because all is energy and resonance. This energy expresses itself through ten different vibrations or emanations that we recognize on the Tree of Life as the Ten Sefirot. To connect with these vibrations is to connect with the creative energy that shapes the universe. On the path of Kabbalah, we seek to know the mind of God, which reveals itself in these ten vibrations. This mind is like a matrix of all matter, for all matter originates and exists only because of energy and the intelligence that is inherent in it (diagram N).

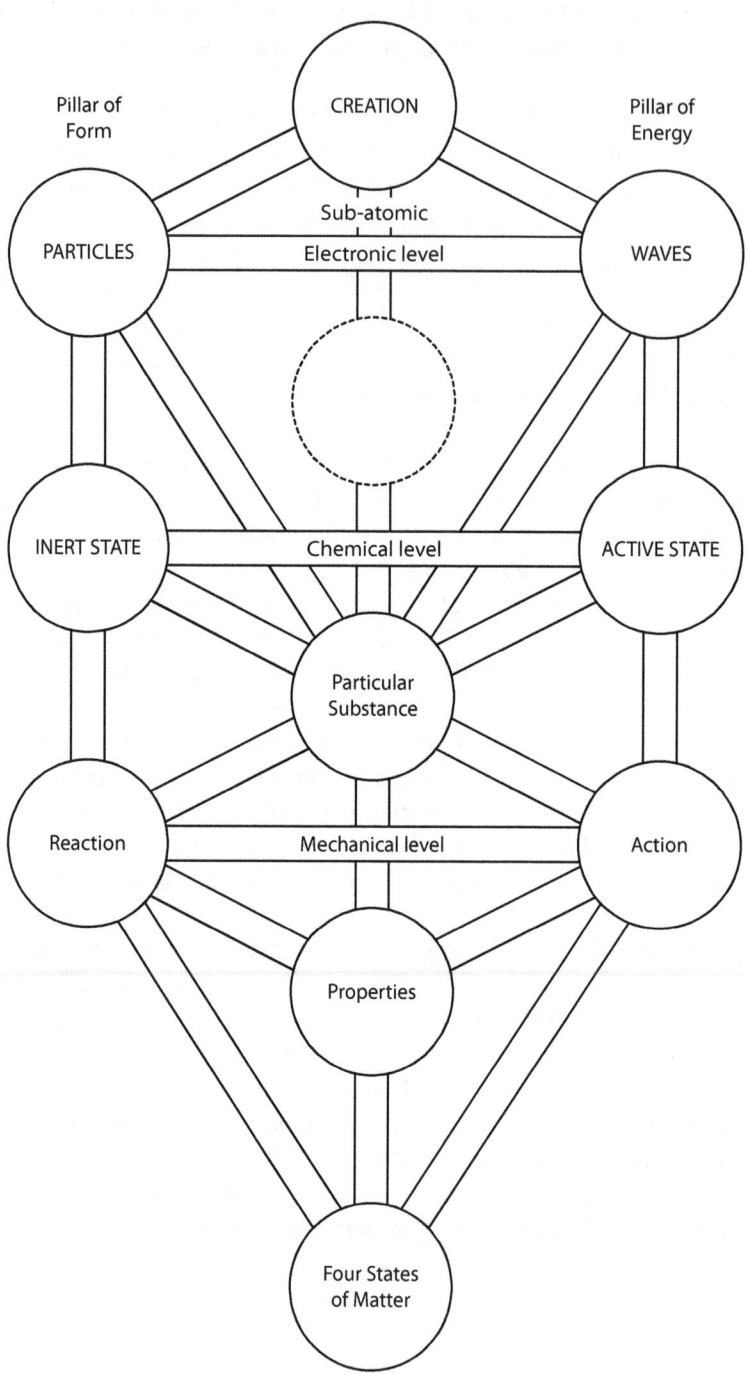

Diagram M

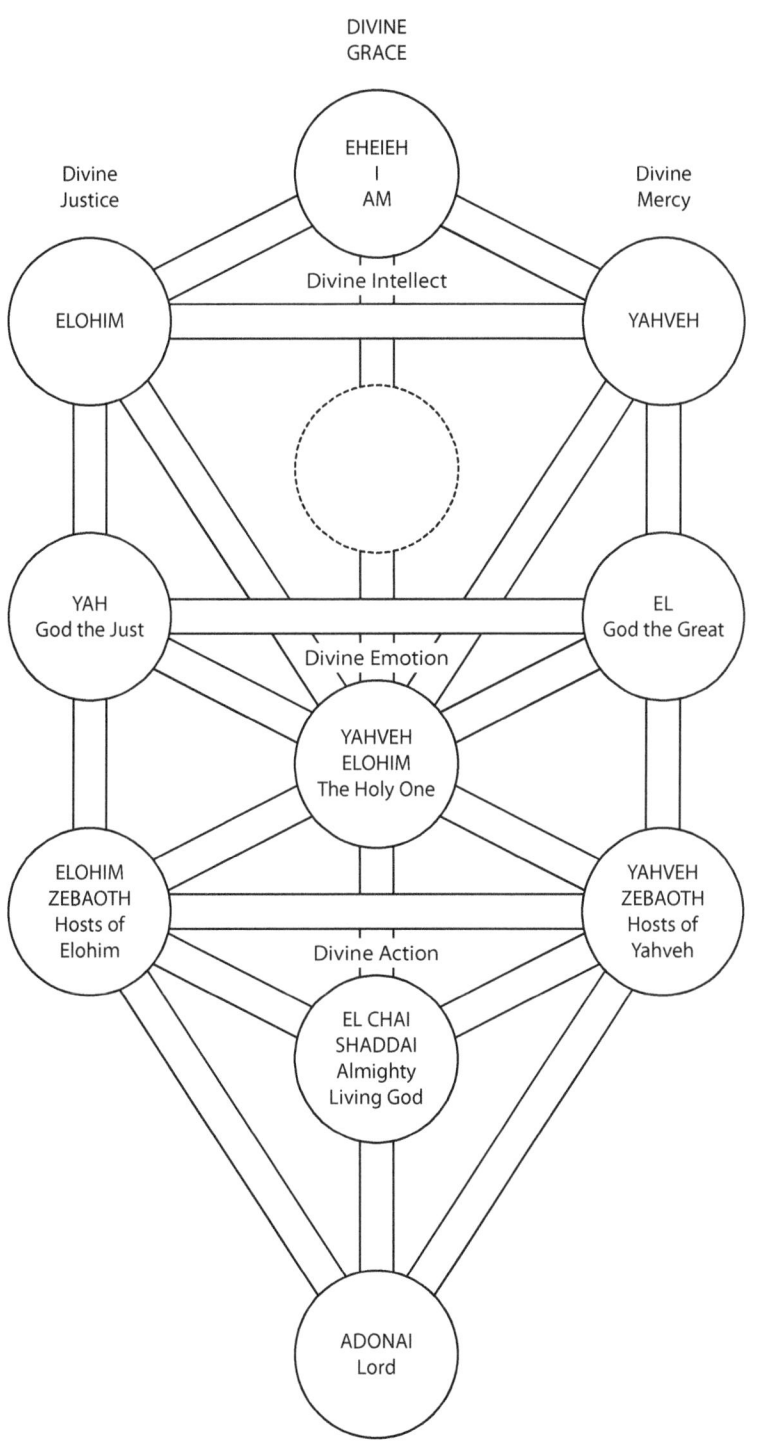

Diagram N

Chapter 13: The causal ability of consciousness within the soul

Mystically, we speak here about 'consciousness that is conscious of being conscious, or the awareness of awareness itself, from which comes the mystical experience that the Universe (in great and small) is a self-aware Being.'

Aziluth or Divine consciousness is the potential to be. It is 'naked consciousness', completely whole and undivided (individual). The soul is a reflection in the psyche, of this consciousness in reflected and relative existence. The soul as the silent witness or observer from the 'Seat of Solomon' knows through sheer 'being-ness'. Consciousness is the experience of the soul, bringing human awareness into the realm of that world of potential and probabilities that the free will of the soul may choose from. The soul has been described in many different ways in esoteric traditions, mediating between mind and matter, and between the higher and lower worlds. These are the upper and lower faces on the Tree of Life respectively. The self-observation from the soul leads to a realization or at least to the fundamental question: who is observing? God looks through the eyes of the soul into the universe, who looks back at Who–Is–Looking!

Who or what is looking through my eyes, listening through my ears, and acting through these hands? The answer may come through different levels of experience, depending on who is answering. On the middle pillar, the Sefirot tell us about who is answering and from what world. From the level of the soul, the transpersonal dimension opens up, and the veil of the first heaven (Malkuth of Briah) separates. Although mindful of the Tree of Assiah, the awareness of who is looking changes into the perspective that it is not 'me' (person or Yesod-ego) who is observing. One discovers that human consciousness is truly the consciousness of the Divine, looking into the world.

All the senses, thoughts, and feelings are potential doorways of consciousness for the Divine to observe itself. This brings us to the physics of possibilities, bringing the paradigm into our awareness that this consciousness, like a conjunction, opens the veil that presents our separateness. The door into the soul literally opens a world of endless possibilities in free choice (diagram I).

Meditation/exercise
You can do this meditation sitting or lying down, but equally make this a walking meditation. Whatever form you select, stay with your senses open to the world around you. Be aware of what you are seeing, hearing, feeling, smelling, and tasting. Thoughts and feelings are all welcome. Let them arise as they come, and let them go as they disappear. Any impression and experience from the inside or outside is allowed.

Now, ask yourself the question: 'Who is aware of all these impressions' or 'who is it that watches these phenomena come and go?'
There is a presence within you that observes these processes like a spectator in a theatre. Be still and let that consciousness arise within you. Be aware now that this consciousness is the Divine looking through your eyes, into its own creation.

Free will
Free choice or free will is where potentiality and possibility become actuality through self-consciousness. Free will is therefore the agent of Divine manifestation. For the question arises out of this experience: Who is choosing? If the answer to the question is: 'I am', coming from the inner experience of the silent witness, there is a presence that testifies to the existence of the world. As such we become the 'eyes, ears, and hands of God'. This 'observer effect' causes waves of possibility to collapse into a particle reality on the subatomic level, manifesting consciousness into concrete and solid form. Through this process of 'wave becoming particle', the subject creates and generates an object.

In Kabbalah, we speak of the first day of creation or light in the Kether of Briah, where there is still no time-space as we know it. Out of the stillness comes movement (time) in the Chocmah of Briah, the Cosmic energy followed by space, the Binah of Briah. This is the level of the second day of creation. Kabbalistic cosmology explains the collapse from wave into particle, through the energy of Chocmah, taking on shape and form in the particle of Binah. This all happens under the observation or the consciousness of Kether, the observing Light.

Human consciousness and the created object then become separate, and the experience of duality is born. Only when the observer remains aware of 'who is looking' shall the subject and object remain an undivided whole without leading to a dualistic inner universe (diagram O).

Outer objects may be created through the wave-collapse (Chocmah) into a particle-form (Binah) coming from the subject-observer, but still, the created object is never separate from the subject. This is the exact process that Kabbalah describes in its cosmology, how the Holy One calls forth the worlds into manifestation and how they are created, formed, and made by an act of will (Kav). The worlds that emanate from Aziluth (Kether of Yezirah, Tifareth of Briah, and Malkuth of Aziluth) are a reflection of the original world of Aziluth, where all is held in the undivided consciousness of the Divine. Even if our being lives from the worlds of creation, formation, and action, the world of Aziluth is always there as the potential from which the manifest world (time-space-movement) comes forth, from moment to moment (from Eternity to Eternity). It is from this place on Jacob's Ladder where the lesser Yaweh or Metatron resides; out of the Godhead or the Eternal, that time-wave and space-particle flow forth into movement (diagram A).

The experience as incarnated beings into time-space-movement is unavoidable and allows us to identify with the wave-particle world as 'moving and concrete'. It can be seen as moving because of the wave effect in the manifested world, and concrete because of the particle effect. The whole elementary-physical world consists of movement and concreteness, as we so vividly come to know in Assiah. Our own physical body and its sensory perceptions, together with the lower psyche (upper part of Yezirah), invite us to observe ourselves and the world around us as dualistic and separate.
In other words, we become enchanted, as it were, by the world of phenomena, which is truly not just an object, but a living creation of the Divine consciousness that looks through the eyes of the soul.

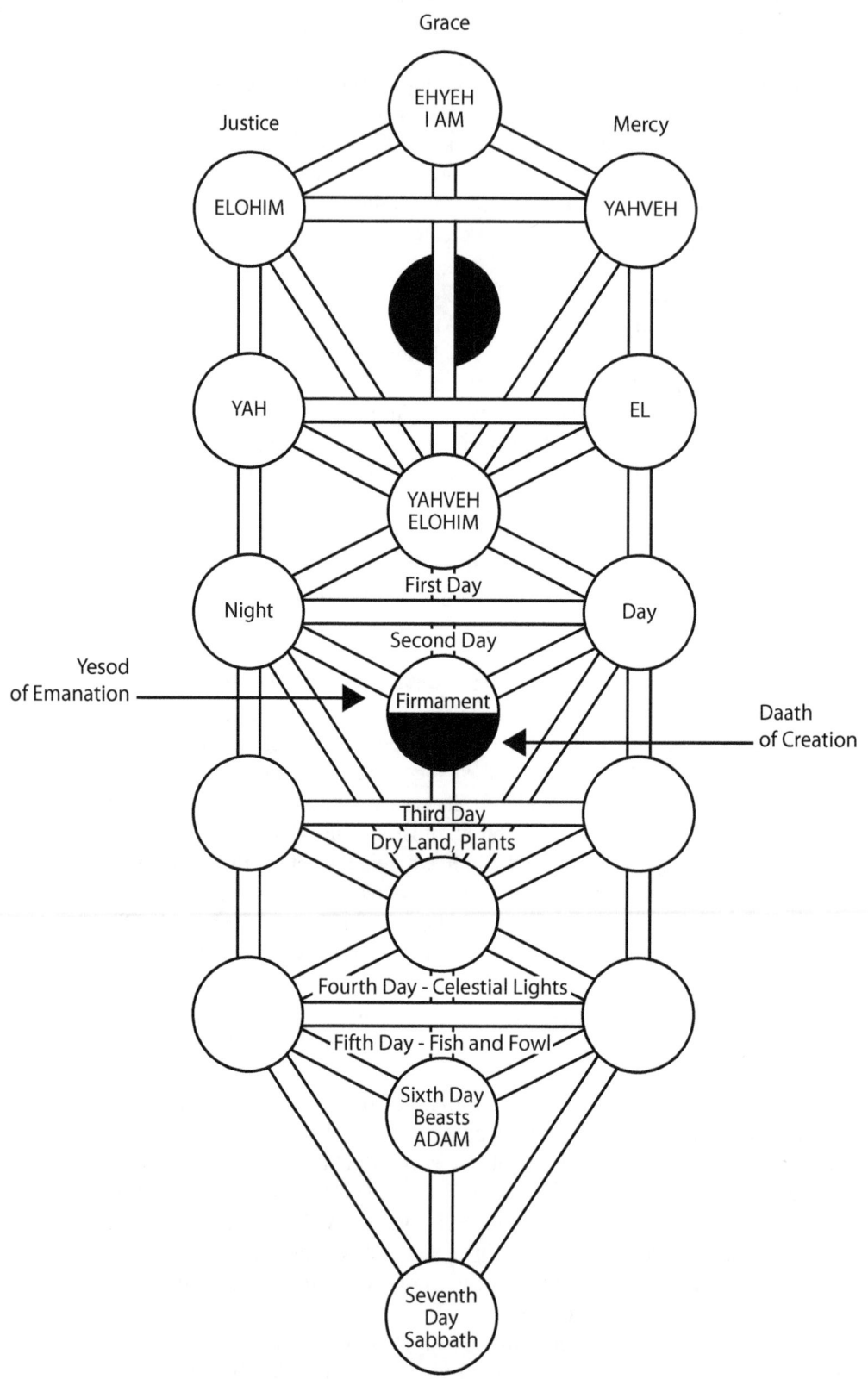

Diagram O

Difficult as it may be to understand, we are truly a co-creator within this cosmic potential, with the world of living phenomena around us and a body that consists of the same components. The irony behind this is that only from that silent-witness perspective, wherein lies free will, can we participate in this creative act. Consciousness is the ground of being (Aziluth), thus a sea of potential, wherefrom all arises and returns.

The more we identify with consciousness at the heart of existence (Tifareth), the more we become aware of this origin, rather than simply being sleep-walking creatures. This changes our sense and experience of space-time from a linear and limited form of time-space, towards an eternal sense of being within space-time. In other words, the Eternal is Aziluth, and the worlds below are the evolving worlds of space-time (all three worlds with their own distinct space-time experience).

It is said in quantum physics that pure consciousness or eternity is without signal, because it has nothing to do with time-space. Yet, it is the 'background' as it were, from which time-space-movement derives and develops. Meanwhile, eternity is free from time-space-movement, communicating without signal and without destination/designated locality. Eternity is eternity. It is all things simultaneously. This suggests that communication from the time-space-less domain of the silent witness-observer is eternal and therefore nonlocal/omnipresent (diagram N).

Meditation

Sit down and relax. Become aware of your breathing and draw your attention into yourself. Bring yourself into the very center of your being, where you rest upon a single point of light. Imagine that you draw all that you are and what you have become into this point of light. Let past and future disappear in the place of peace and stillness where you are.

When you reach this consciousness, you arrive at the knowledge of being the Eternal and existing in the nonlocal domain, where time and space have not yet developed but rest in the potential of eternity.

Within you lives the Spirit of eternity, while time, space, and movement are lying within, waiting to unfold out of you. With the next breath let time-space and movement flow out of your being.

Be at peace with how eternity has expressed itself into the movement of the universe and your breath.

Chapter 14: Quantum physics and creation

So, these Quantum-Kabbalah metaphysics explain something about God and even more about the universe and the human being. Potentially, as a human being (Adam Kadmon), we are complete, as nothing could be added unto us. Yet, human beings are feverishly seeking the things they lack or don't possess. This situation is caused by the final manifestation of consciousness into matter, which has caused the enchantment (illusion) of the human being identifying with matter and one's psychological (Yesod of Yezirah) identity. Through this identity with matter, different verbs expressing the relationship between identity and matter came into being. These verbs are 'to have' and 'to desire', which in some cases result in the human problem of: 'I desire what I don't have'. This in turn leads to an endless search for the unattainable, as the 'hunger' for what we do not have in our possession is never satisfied.

Imagine a classroom full of children, and the teacher says that today the Holy One will come to visit and each child may ask for something. They all have individual desires for those things that they don't have. One wishes for a new bike, others an infinite sweet supply, a bigger room, new parents, etc. The teacher is amazed and says, 'Boys and girls, I cannot believe that you are asking for all these superficial things. Why don't you ask for intelligence? That is what I would wish'. A boy stands up and responds, 'Well, we all wish for something we don't have'!

Quantum creativity is participation in the process of creation from the quantum level of consciousness present at the heart of the human being, the soul. The lower psychological consciousness, corresponding to the lower face of the Tree of Yezirah, is not called forth, created, and formed to create, but to generate and regenerate. If the psyche were in a perpetual state of creation, the human being would bring forth new ideas without any conscious consideration or discernment. Looking at the current state of our human development, that would lead to great chaos. The lower face is occupied with (re)generation of old conditionings, while the upper face is the place of true creativity (not what some like to think of as creativity).

Metaphysics like this brings me to another story. In this age of tremendous scientific progression and development, the most brilliant and smart minds of the scientific world gathered to discuss the current state of affairs. As they could make a sheep, a cow, and even a human embryo in test tubes in a laboratory, they decide to arrange a meeting with God, to tell Him that he is no longer needed. The date and time is set, and they are in front of the great Creator, advising Him, in a respectful way, that He is dismissed from further duty in the universe. God says to them, 'Well, that is fine, I see your point, but what makes you think that you can replace me?' The scientists respond that they can make life in their laboratory and offer to make a human out of the clay of the earth. They want to start immediately, but God stops them and says, 'No, no, first make the clay!'

There are four conditions that quantum physics suggests are the ingredients for creation:
- Downward causation
- Non-locality
- Discontinuity
- Tangled hierarchy

All four conditions must be engaged in the creative process, otherwise, the creative act would not be accomplished. The choice-consciousness in the world of Assiah is simply too insufficient and limited, thus causing a collapse out of the realm of endless consciousness and possibilities. Within the ideas of modern psychology and science, the 'mind' and the brain are often synonymous with each other. Nothing could be further from the truth.

In addition, the mind is not merely an epiphenomenon of the brain. The intellect we see on the Tree and Jacob's Ladder is situated at the higher face of Yezirah/ lower face of Briah. The intellect is more located within the transpersonal and universal domain, wherein we find the cultural concepts and age-old memories of humanity. The brain is located at the Malkuth of Yezirah and does not create the mind. What it does do is generate thoughts, and these thoughts are entangled with the brain (diagram B and G).

What entanglement means in this example is that there can be no thoughts without the brain, but correspondingly there can be no brain without thoughts. Consciousness holds both within its embrace. As both brain and thought are interdependent, they connect and collapse simultaneously. When brain becomes thought, thought becomes brain.

Potentiality and actuality are intrinsically entangled in the domain of non-locality. It is only in the domain of relativity (time-space-movement) that we can distinguish between the subject and the object, as both being someone whilst simultaneously beholding the separate world as an object.

We could say that 'potential' and 'actual' are the opposites of one another when they collapse, but they are in fact never separate; the unconscious and consciousness are opposite each other as well.

Chapter 15: Supramental and archetypal

In some esoteric and quantum-scientific sources, the word supramental is used to describe being above or on a higher octave than mental. Mental, as we have seen, relates to the lower Yezirah and the personal domain of the psyche, with the Yesod of Yezirah at its center—the ego and personality. The lower face of the Yeziratic world contains three levels within the mental state: mineral, vegetable, and animal (diagram G).

These lower mental states correspond with the three lower chakras, Muladhara, Swadisthana, and Manipura, exactly mirroring the mineral, vegetable, and animal states of consciousness respectively. The supramental level can be found on the Tree of the psyche, on the upper face, interlocking with the lower face of Briah and therefore with the collective unconscious. We know this as the realm of the archetypes and which was discussed in chapter eleven. These supramental states correspond with the three upper chakras and the three upper heavens on Jacob's Ladder (diagram P).

In between these two faces or gardens on the Tree, we find the crucial place of Tifareth and the soul. This is the place of self-consciousness and free will. Our Tifareth resonates with the Anahata chakra, the place of transformation and creativity, from the lower mental states into the higher supramental states. In other words, from generative states to creative states.
It can be seen in diagram Q that the supramental states in metaphysics are called 'Heavens' and are states or stages of transpersonal awareness. These three higher states or heavens are sublimated states of the three lower chakras or natural states. It is important to understand that the so-called lower levels are reflections of the higher levels, essential to be able to function in the natural world.

In other words, the archetypal content that comes to us through the collective unconscious has transformative abilities, carrying metaphysical wisdom that we experience as spiritual morals, emotions, and values. From this upper realm of Yezirah comes a deeper and profound understanding of our innate nobility and vitality, which is very distinct from our normal, daily life. The reason for this is that within the triad of the Spirit on the Tree, we find the Holy Spirit (Ruach Ha-Kadosh), inspiring and vitalizing all who draw near.

In this higher face on the Tree of Life, we may also come into contact with fundamental creativity, a universal creativity that resonates with the process of how creation came into being. Fundamental is an appropriate term at this level of the Spirit, as it is located at the Yesod of Briah/Daath of Yezirah. The title for this emanation (Yesod) is 'Foundation' and therefore brings a clue to the cosmic mode of creativity, which is truly creative and different from 'situational creativity' that we profess from the lower face of Yezirah.

The difference between fundamental and situational creativity lies with the fact that situational means to generate from old and already existent concepts. For example: a musician may compose a new song, but it is always based upon melodies that are already in existence.

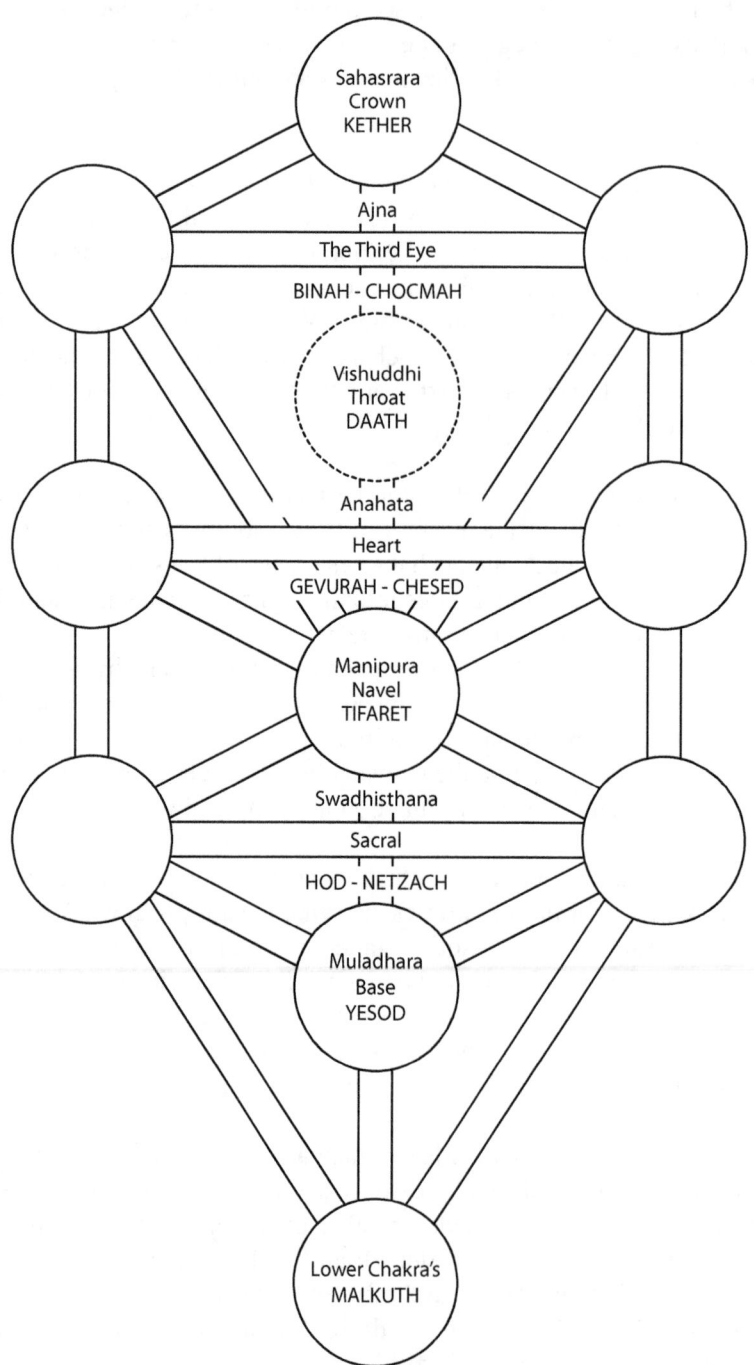

Diagram P

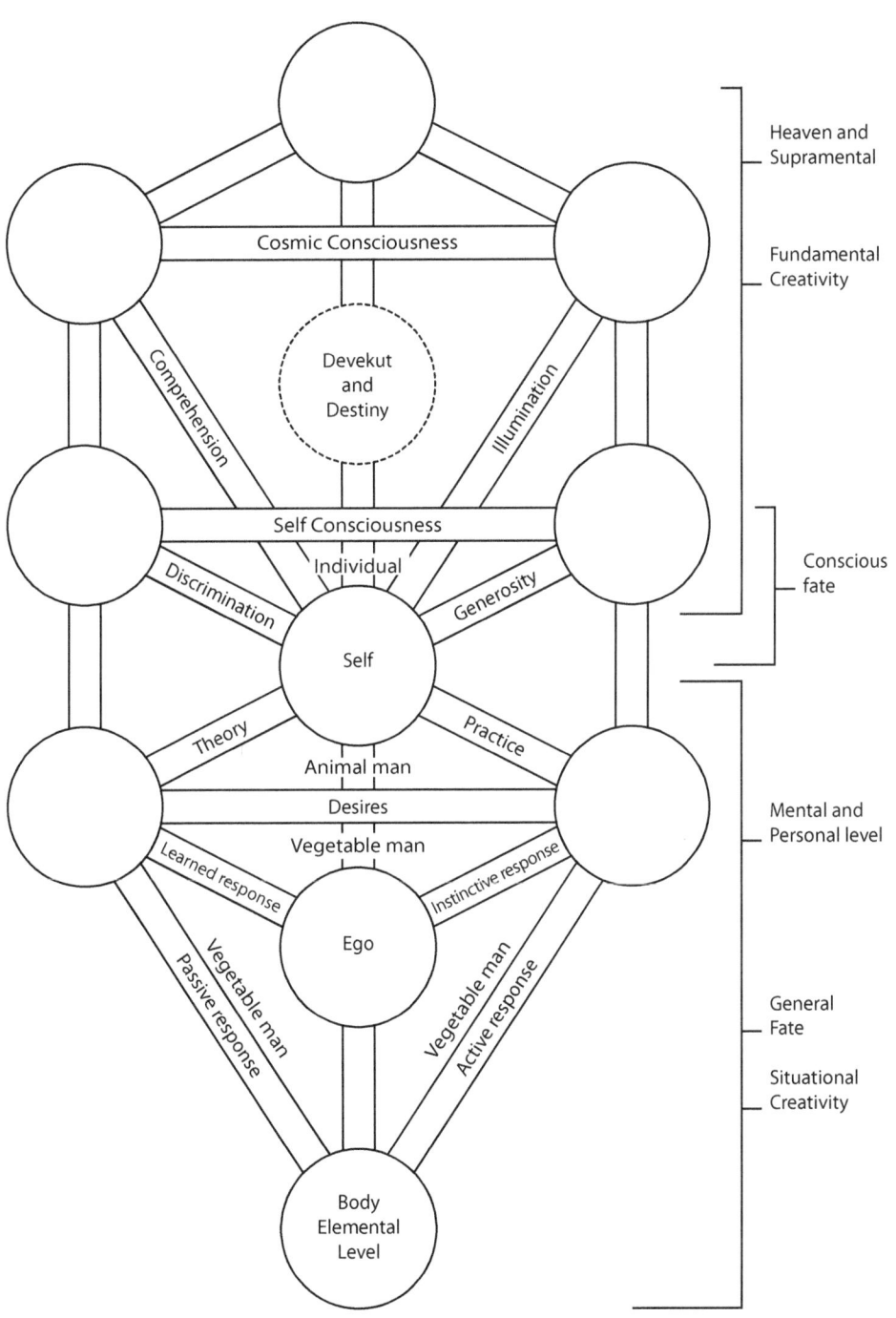

Diagram Q

To be completely original, which is indeed possible through fundamental creativity, one does not invent a whole new tone-scale, but creates a melody that was previously non-existent. The same can be done by a painter, an architect, a writer, or any person who has an inspiration coming from the upper Yezirah.

To be in-spirited or inspired means to participate within this consciousness where the archetypal/collective unconscious resides. For the Kabbalist this is not a matter of 'work' but a readiness, an openness, or what I like to call 'availability' towards Spirit. The Wisdom and Understanding coming from the Daath of Yezirah is a gift rather than a product of work. A matter of grace rather than merit (diagram Q).

Chapter 16: Four worlds

Out of the four stages of Divine unfoldment come forth the four stages of consciousness and four modes of perceiving existence. All in all, these comprise four ways for the soul to let God look unto Its own existence.

The primal world of Aziluth, the origin of pure, naked consciousness, where all four potentialities previously discussed are present in potential or within four states of possibility:
1. Consciousness (Divine) - Aziluth
2. Supramental - Briah
3. Mental and Vital - Yezirah
4. Physical - Assiah

The four perceptions are known in Kabbalah as the mystical, metaphysical, symbolic, and literal respectively (diagram A). In addition, these levels can be described as love, intuition, thinking/feeling, and sensing. The worlds of Assiah and Yezirah (lower face) contain the natural world and as such, the natural human being (Adam Kadmon in the world of Assiah). These comprise the shared natural levels of mineral, vegetable, and animal life with the senses and the vital (energetic) thought, mental, and memory functions. As complex as the natural human being is, there is much more if we consider the role of Jacob's Ladder within, seeing that this is exactly and only one of four worlds.

The physical and the mental-vital levels are in proximity to each other, corresponding to the natural and outer world respectively, thus attuning a part of our inner world with the outer world. This is the way we perceive and engage with our environment.

Mental and supramental are one and the same world (Yezirah), differentiated into lower and upper faces, within the respective personal and transpersonal domains of operation. In between these two faces, the soul keeps watch. These two parts of the same world are distinct and different, but are intrinsically related to one another. While the lower part is occupied with personal and psychological development, consisting of a general fate, the upper Yezirah is transpersonal, where insights of one's destiny are received.

General or unconscious fate is the personal pattern that develops through living directly and participating within the world of Assiah. From there we are received at birth and immediately invited to follow the patterns and examples of our personal milieu and culture. There is a strong tendency to influence and be influenced on the vegetable level from this lower psychological level at the lower face of Yezirah/upper face of Assiah. Life here is like a reflection of all the things surrounding us, and as such we are shaped and formed in accordance with the environment.

General fate therefore not only is personal, but entails a collective or group fate, giving direction and movement to the deep unconscious of that group. Most people think (or like to think) that they are uninfluenced by this process, but no one can escape the vast pressure that comes from the collective-general fate which moves us. It moves both the masses and the individual within it (diagram Q).

From this Yeziratic dynamic, located at the lower face of this world, we can easily see why there is no such thing as 'fundamental creativity' but only reflective or 'situational creativity'. Besides observing this process, the soul is the place of self-consciousness and the seat of free will. The soul observes and scrutinizes the ego. One becomes the silent witness, perceiving oneself as a part of the totality, while the Yesod-ego can only observe part of itself in relation to the physical body and the social environment. As a result of this dawning awareness of the soul and its intricate possibilities, the soul notices that the general fate is not 'written in stone' and can be changed and even transformed.

The soul is where we start to observe the dynamic consequences in ourselves and around us concerning general fate. First we awaken to participation in our general fate from the awakening triad of the animal level. We see the influence of parents, grandparents, family, school, education, friends, work, religion, and society.

Choices can be made that bring oneself out of the psychological territory of the social-emotional pressure that keeps the vegetable level in control, preventing it from growing and developing. This is described as the specific or individual fate, differentiating oneself from the group and initiating the self-liberating process of practicing free will. Life moves from the sphere of activity (karma or mazal) with Yesod at its centre towards the second sphere on the Tree, with Tifareth at its center: the sphere of growth (diagram G).

As discussed previously, the upper part of the Tree of Yezirah and lower Briah is the place of the archetypal-collective unconscious where we find the transpersonal dimension, making the greater pattern available to us, that extends over lifetimes. Here we are introduced to our destiny, exploring higher values and morals, meaning the place we have in the world and the specific task that we have developed and followed (conscious or unconsciously) over many lifetimes. Awakening to our destiny always leaves space for our free will, meaning that one is not obliged or forced to follow destiny. However, most individuals find that the path is intertwined with one's feelings of bliss and being whole. As Spirit guides us on the path of destiny, we feel inspired, challenged, comforted, tested, grateful, and stimulated to persevere along the path of awe (from Tifareth to Kether). Finding meaning, purpose, and a spiritual direction in life gives the human soul a place to 'rest its head'. Some call it a homecoming.

Out of this contact with the higher world of Briah erupts an inner creativity that expresses itself in many different forms. In the expressions of the deeper life, the essential meaning of the Sefirot comes to the surface. These expressions are well defined in many pieces of art, music, poetry, and architecture. The spiritual virtues of the creative world can find their way into the lower vehicle of the natural worlds. This can only happen if the soul has guided the lower vehicle into processes of purification in order to prepare it for reception.

This inner mode or stature departs from Tifareth, the self which has contact with soul. This particular state or Gadlut is the awareness of silent witness, called 'sitting on the seat of Solomon' in Kabbalah. For most skilled and trained Kabbalists, it is a virtue to be able to enter this state at will, but they leave the Gadlut state as soon as the ego consciousness (Katnut) engages with the worldly affairs.

The more one is able to remain in this higher state of Gadlut, the more we are available to and reliable for the Spirit (triad Tifareth-Binah-Chocmah). This is known as Devekut or the 'cleaving unto God'. The inner or fundamental creativity is born out of love or unity (Aziluth). From the human side (natural world and the soul), the Kabbalist starts choosing from the archetypal content of the upper Yezirah, instead of reproducing old choices based on memories and former experiences. But what does this actually mean?

Archetypes are the essential principles that give rise to the worlds of form and ultimately to the physical world. If one shifts from living the personal life based on automatic reactions (vegetable level), and aspires for the archetypal life, they begin living from self-consciousness, free will, creative freedom, spiritual insights, and inspiration. In mythological texts, the archetypes are the gods, angels, demons, and other beings who express the higher creative energies that are the actual structure of the world we live in. They are the personifications of the creative principles of Briah.

These forces bring transformation, setting the world of form and action into motion. In the word trans-formation we can see the meaning of what really changes: namely, the lower face of the world of Yezirah and the personal structure that we have constructed. Of course the world itself does not change, nor do the psychological principles that make up the metaphysics on the Tree of Life. What does change and transform, however, from working within the archetypal domain, is the personal structure that we regard as 'ourselves' (diagram Q).

Another important distinction between the natural world and the higher Briatic world is the experience of time. The natural world and the lower psyche experience the world as continuous in time, while on the higher archetypal level, the experience is discontinuous.

It is only through the frequencies that our physical senses detect and the way that the lower psyche works (through memory) that we know the world around us and ourselves as continuous. The ego likes to think that it is continuous or immortal by placing itself central to all activities. From the perspective of the soul, the body and the ego are discontinuous and mortal, but the consciousness that observes these mortal phenomena, i.e., the soul, is itself immortal and discontinuous.

The soul knows that it needs conscious intention (Kavanah) in order to be creative. We can will all we want, even using free will, but will is a moment in time that loses its focus, strength, and potential if there is no intention to support it.

Ego-consciousness knows about time in a linear sense by looking backwards and forwards. Within the scope of this linear view, there is limited range, because we look from the eyes of the Yesod-ego. This is what is called the 'arrow of time', drawing time in a linear and simultaneous fashion. Darwinism is such a way of describing evolution, where there is no space for fundamental creativity based on the quantum-physics paradigm that the creative world is discontinuous.

Knowing that consciousness in the natural world does not readily evolve towards quantum-creative states of consciousness, we do not make use of it much if at all, leaving Darwinism as a continuous theory, dependent on the interpretation of fossil records and linear ideas of logic and thought.

Notice that 'logic' coming from certain concepts of the mental (lower Yezirah) world is by definition not creative, but linear and continuous.

So, how does conscious purpose get into matter or become matter? It can only do so by free choice and intention, whilst choosing from within the fundamental-creative domain. This is the domain of the archetypal-collective unconscious wherefrom inspiration is derived. The complete natural Tree of Life (Assiah) is not simply designed to be creative, but to reproduce, repeat, form, adapt, change, and anticipate natural conditions. The cosmic creative world influences the natural world constantly, yet the natural world cannot 'lift itself by its own arm'. Meaning that the microcosm, through its inability to create, does not move or change anything in the higher worlds.

Having said all this, in Kabbalah and quantum physics the worlds are not separate from each other, although they may be portrayed as such (even on the Kabbalistic diagram of Jacob's Ladder). The stars, the planets, the gods, archangels, and angels all exist in unity within the earth's sphere. The universe is not 'out there' but right here. Not only are you and the whole planet in the universe, but you are the universe. The cosmic plane that we call the fundamental creative level or Briah is within and around us. The potential for creativity and the cosmic ability to transform and perform miracles is within you and everybody else (diagram H).

Until this world is (re)discovered within yourself, we are confined and locked within the lower worlds of reproduction and action. It is a part of the Kabbalistic work to find the Heavens within and bring them to earth. How do we remember these worlds in and around us? For remembering is exactly what we need. It was said during the slavery period of the people of Israel, 'Forgetfulness is suffering, but remembrance is liberation'.

Through making gradual contact with our soul, as discussed above, in meditation and moving into stillness, one will receive the fundamental properties of the soul. Being the silent witness and knower of the process of life. Let us now look closer into this domain.

Chapter 17: Soul and reincarnation

There are many philosophical concepts in the east and west that attempt to explain reincarnation. Could it make matters more complicated to discuss this topic and attempt to combine it with quantum physics and Kabbalah? Definitely!

Nonetheless, the whole natural Tree or world of Assiah/lower face Yezirah has the ability to incarnate, and all that incarnates will eventually discarnate or move back to where it came from. The physical body disintegrates into the elemental parts from which it was constructed, and the lower Yeziratic vehicle decomposes, leaving no trace of the personality and the ego structure that came together with the physical body. Both are constructions of the world of Assiah and Yezirah. All that is built from these worlds will return back where it came from.

The cycles move according to law, arranging the manifested worlds as they are called forth and created into being. They are formed and made, returning to their proper place, for nothing is lost or wasted in the universe.

In this sense, the universe and life itself are indeed immortal, changing their form and substance, but the unchangeable or Aziluth remains constant throughout this process. Physical and mental experiences, i.e., the physiological and lower psychological-ego experience are for the greater part stored as personal, mental memories, or in other words as 'brain memories'. These memories can be traced back through recalling events and other personal conditionings. On the Tree, we find such memories in the lower circle with Yesod, the personal unconscious, at its center (diagram G).

We build this memory gradually, passing through the stages of our life with the major influences that come to us from the outside world. Without choice, constructed experiences and memories are facilitated for the most part through the exterior conditions. The way we react to the world, our interior response to circumstances and people, is very subjective and personal. Although we live in a very impersonal cosmic universe, we make our life very personal, related through memory.

This memory will not last; it remains only for the time our physical life is sustained on this earth and disintegrates after physical death. However, the memories that are unconscious reflections of a personal life can become conscious when they are brought into the life-processing orbit of the soul.

The realm of Yesod of Yezirah is a vast memory-bank containing what is learned, sensed, and felt. It is an amalgam of impressions and images woven together into a type of personal timeline-timeframe where we find reference between an inner and an outer life. As discussed previously in chapter seven, we call this place on the Tree and Jacob's Ladder 'the Treasure House of Images'.

There are a few good reasons why this name was given. Firstly because Yesod is related to the esoteric principle of the moon, reflecting thoughts, ideas, images, and all memories that have been accumulated in a lifespan thus far. Secondly, the reflection shows a passive type of memory that mirrors back at us what once was.

Once one becomes discarnate, the mirror reflects once more, showing us the story of our lifetime, after it shatters and disintegrates. Beyond the mirror and the world of Assiah, the soul is operative as the vehicle of consciousness. It is through this seat of consciousness that one comes into contact with and allows the Holy One to look through one's eyes and hear through one's ears.

In other words; the free will, which is spoken about so extensively in esoteric circles, has the choice to turn towards the higher world of Briah or bury itself in the worldly affairs of Assiah. The soul positions itself at the very center of the Tree, enabling the human being to connect 'heaven to earth'.

Such experiences are of a different psycho-spiritual order, taken and carried within the vessel of the soul towards the next incarnation. In the imagination, we can visualize this journey as a movement or migration from life a to life b.

Let us not forget, however, that consciousness itself has no properties other than presence, stillness, and wakeful observation or the silent witness. These inner qualities give the human being the experience 'to be in the world, but not of it', finding oneself free of time-space awareness, whilst living in the world of time-space-movement. In Kabbalah, this would be described as being conscious of timelessness or eternity within time-space.

Meditation/exercise
Sit in meditation and become aware of the body that you inhabit. Ask yourself the question: Is it the body you inhabit or is the body inhabiting you? Start to breathe consciously and ask yourself the question: Who is breathing? Let the breath move completely by itself and ask yourself the question: Are you breathing or are you breathed?

Observe your thoughts, aware of the ever-flowing stream of thoughts that pass through your mind. Do not exclude these thoughts, merely let them be. Let them rise and fall in your consciousness. Ask yourself where these thoughts come from. Are you born out of thought or does thought come forth out of you?

Feel the energy in yourself. What quality can you perceive in the energies within you? See where they come from. What is their source?

Slowly become aware that it is you who knows all these things. That you are in a world that is coming forth out of you.

The soul therefore has these timeless properties while being in the world, thus being in this life and beyond. The esoteric-quantum idea comes from the knowledge that the soul does not incarnate again, nor does it migrate according to this challenging paradigm where Kabbalah and quantum physics meet. Instead, the soul remembers the individual life-processes it has undergone over one or many lifetimes.

We could compare this remembering to waking up in the morning and bringing the dream into waking (Yesod) consciousness. From there, it is possible to not only recall, but also integrate the dream into daily life. To incarnate is to wake up from the dream that was our former incarnation. For most of humankind, the lives lived fade away partly or completely at birth, depending on the spiritual development in past lives. It is the maturity of the soul and the complete human vehicle as a whole self in a former lifetime that allow us to re-member what we were, where we are, and where we are moving towards (fate and destiny).

The challenging esoteric hypothesis in this book suggests that the soul does not migrate but is indeed a vessel of consciousness that rests within the timeless dimension, wherefrom life is born and will return (Aziluth). For this reason, it is from the soul that the spiritual experiences speak to us, giving us evidential knowledge of the spiritual (Briatic) and Divine realms (Aziluth).

The knowledge (Daath) does not 'move', but it is an omnipresent constant, like a memory in daily life that you remember wherever you are. Quantum physics refers to quantum memory that consists of a non-local and therefore timeless confluence of memories that 'carry' or contain specific thoughts and images that lie in our individual karmic pattern.

Chapter 18: Purpose

Purpose comes in various forms and shapes according to human intention and needs. Most of us have a purpose in life that has something to do with happiness and fulfilment of needs. It depends upon where the need or desire comes from, whether it is easily satisfied, or if it will return in time, for every need and desire returns sooner or later.

The urge to continuously satisfy the needs and desires in life, one's purpose, makes the human restless and in endless pursuit of a purpose that will never be truly satisfied. Purpose is located on the Tree of Life in the Divine triad of Kether-Chocmah-Binah. Here we find the principle of what a human being sees and regards as a crown on one's destiny. In other words: if that purpose is achieved, life itself is the true meaning. Some say, 'I came to earth to fulfill this specific task' (purpose).

Purpose and meaning are intrinsically intertwined in the human story, for there is no other creature that we know of that works and moves towards purpose. Of course, it is quite a different purpose if one departs in life from Malkuth, Yesod, Tifareth, or even higher on the middle pillar of the Tree of Life. Purpose and meaning shift according to the level or stage of consciousness one is at, illustrated by the progression of consciousness and spiritual development up the central pillar (diagram R).

Purpose at the higher Divine triad on the Tree is different to that on the lower face of the Tree, where we share the common or general fate of humanity. As we approach the soul level, we awaken to self-consciousness, arising with a sense of specific or individual fate. This awareness of our specific or individual fate and destiny then brings us closer to our higher purpose.

It is from this inner domain of the soul, where free will rests, that we are able to cause changes to happen that fall within the scope of quantum selection. Free will opens the possibilities to consciously choose from the quantum field (Briatic). Here the archetypal possibilities exist as principalities or essential beings. In Kabbalah, these archetypes are known as archangels and the Higher Angels (diagram H).

We make decisions from the level of self-consciousness (soul). We have the potential to be truly creative and transformative (spiritual action). It is not uncommon that while the soul starts to perceive the line of destiny, it simultaneously gives more clarity to the purpose at hand.

This realisation is brought to the receptive soul that is inspired to live more and more in accord with higher goals and meanings. It shows that a Divine purpose in life is relative, depending on the evolutionary stage of development on the Tree of Life.

Quantum physics adds to this that if we wish to make a real transformation possible, we need to commence our choosing from higher spiritual principles (Briatic order), e.g., love, justice, harmony, compassion, and strength. The natural human being needs guidance that elevates the natural state into something more and greater.

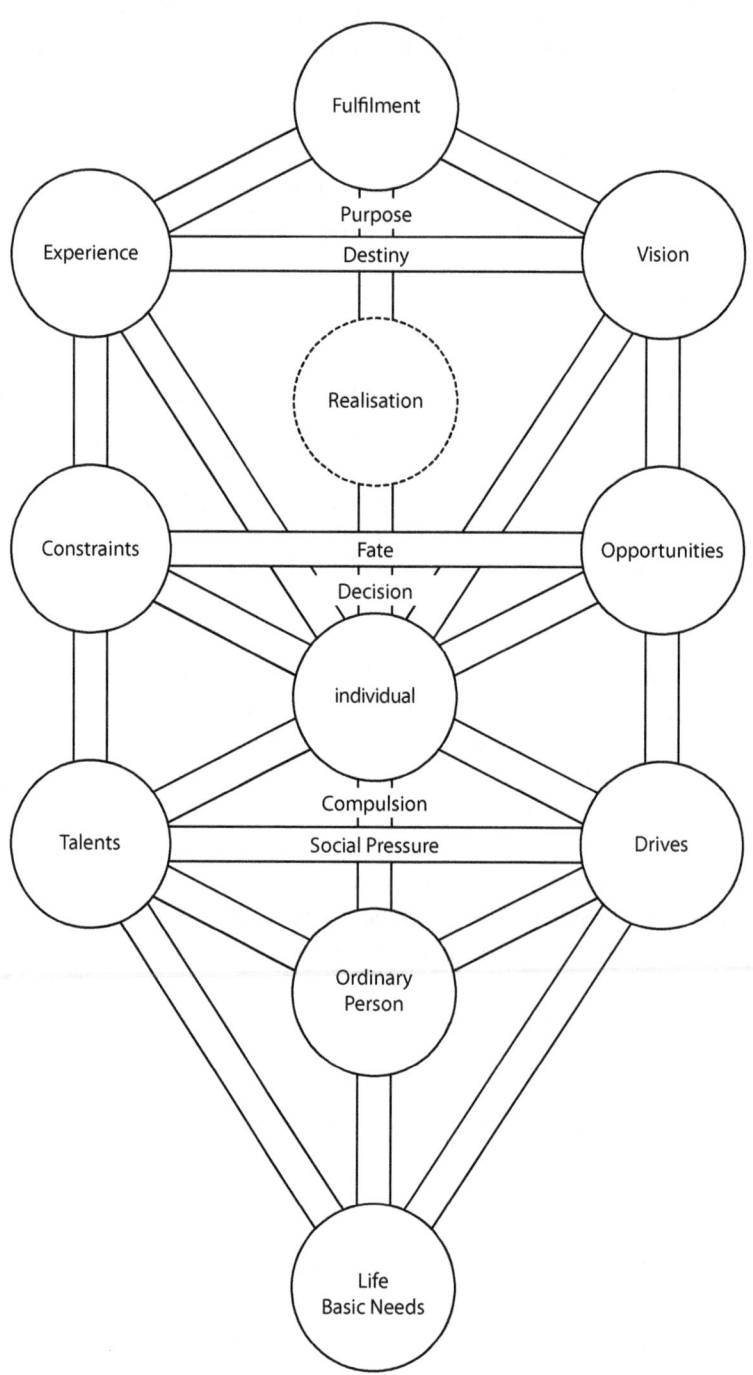

Diagram R

Purpose and karma
How can we distinguish between accumulated memories from a current incarnation and specific karmic memories? What we learn through the contact with the world, the immediate family, culture, and so on are accumulated memories (diagram J). These are not the same memories as karmic memories that are also referred to as quantum memories.

Naturally, these two distinct memory types, the one personal and the other from a transpersonal order, should be integrated and meditated upon. How else, as Kabbalists, do we come to any serious integration and unity of what our transmigrated self has to say about the continuation in a current life? In other words; our present life does matter very much, asking us to remember what we have gathered through other lives, weaving a pattern that is in harmony with our greater spiritual design. This spiritual design is known as destiny, where we come in touch with the inner realization of what it means to be part of a greater structure and Being. Such an insight shows the human being that this life is not about us, as is often explained by our inner mentor or teacher (maggid).

As discussed previously, a clear destiny leads to purpose and meaning of life. Purpose and meaning not only give perspective to our individual existence, but act as functioning beacons that guide us onwards along archetypal principles. Instead of leading our life according to the impulses of the worldly affairs and personal memories, if we have purpose, we consciously follow the inner-symbolic memory that portrays our individual karmic pattern.
This asks for an inquisitive and exploring attitude towards our deeper, unconscious levels (higher Yezirah), where the archetypes present themselves not only as cosmic essences, but as inner personifications of creative and spiritual energy. It is the soul in every human being that sets out on the journey for this unique exploration towards purpose and meaning. It is unique because each individual path is formed by the decisions that one makes, based upon unconscious (generative) or conscious (creative) fate.

Quantum thought and the use of free will open the inner possibilities to create out of the very center of our being: Tifareth. However difficult this is in its abstract form, the true creative act is called a 'creative quantum leap' and can be compared with a discontinuous jump in a continuous time frame.

Imagine that our physical and lower psychological existence is experiencing the world as a time-space-movement continuum. It seems that our body and personal psyche wish to experience this idea and feeling of never-ending life. After all, these parts of the human totality are time-space dependent and will perish in due time. They are both more or less stuck in that stage of consciousness, where they exist in conformity with the natural surroundings we came to live in.

In order to be creative, we need to make a quantum leap in consciousness. After all, the quantum domain is the realm of consciousness (the all potential consciousness of Aziluth). From the light of this consciousness (heart of Aziluth) spring forth the two creative principles of Chocmah (time) and Binah (space) and the world of Briah. The higher creative worlds start to unfold.

Kether is the pure realm of probabilities, while Chocmah and Binah represent the wave and the particle function respectively.

The potential wave in Chocmah, the boundless wisdom in the cosmos, may collapse into a new form or 'particle' in the understanding of Binah. If there is no quantum leap or discontinuity, there will be no true creativity, but only a regeneration of older collapses, a repetition of the same old consciousness and perspective.

To be able to work with a new archetype on the Tree of Life, in this case Tifareth, we direct our intention and energy towards the archetype of the self. Why are archetypes so different from personal symbols and memories? Because they belong to the creative world (collective unconscious) of the transpersonal and metaphysical. Archetypes carry with them the intrinsic capacity (Chocmah and Binah of Briah) to transform life in all its energy and form.

What is needed in order to be creative is to apply consciousness, imagination, and choice (free will). Let us take this a step further, as there are multiple places on the middle pillar on the Tree of Life and Jacob's Ladder that are called Tifareth. Free will lies at the heart of Yezirah and touches the soul triad (free will, processes of life, and conscience), but it is simultaneously the place where the 'three lower worlds meet'.

The Kether of Assiah is the physical maturity we may all grow towards in due time. However, to be knowledgeable of the body (Daath of Assiah) is another matter. This crown on the natural-physical Kingdom means that we are conscious of our physical vehicle (diagram B).

The Tifareth of Yezirah is that psychological self at the center of the world of the psyche. The Malkuth of Briah is called the Kingdom of Heaven. Kingdom because this is Malkuth of the heavenly world of Briah. At the foot of this Briatic world, we step into the Spirit realm and the first heaven. In Kabbalah, this heaven is called 'Vilon' or 'Veil' as it is at this very place we encounter the experience of dawning consciousness that makes us see that we can 'be aware of being aware'. Here is the first glimpse of the quantum self, from which we can freely choose from the wave-like possibilities into a 'collapse' of manifested particles. The opening of the 'Veil' reveals a kind of 'naked consciousness', a self that is truly self-existent without any particular properties.

From this point on the Jacob's ladder, it is possible to occupy a space in consciousness that contains and embraces all three perspectives. Being in that state of naked consciousness, one can simultaneously be in the world of the psyche and the body. That is to say, that spiritual consciousness does not exclude ordinary, daily consciousness. On the contrary, Spirit is all inclusive and therefore contains within it all other, forthcoming consciousness inherent to Spirit. In quantum terms, the quantum self is omnipresent within its own manifested world.

Although it is possible to reach this summit upon one's own inner mountain (on the Tree of Life), it is not so easy to remain there. A nice metaphor we can extend upon is the altitude on the mountain. As we reach higher, the air becomes thinner, moving into the more ethereal realm of Briah (air). The Kingdom of Heaven can be grasped, but it is difficult to hold on to.

We spoke about the state of Gadlut when we attain the summit (place where the three lower worlds meet), but it is only from an established state of Devekut (devotion) that we can find a stable ground in Malkuth of Briah. This is all a matter of inner work and consciousness.

Making the synthesis with quantum physics, we come to an entanglement between the consciousness that creates us and the created forms and beings. We might even come to certain insights that tell us we are co-creators and that the body and the world we live in are self-begotten. Moreover, we give rise to these forms in a creative way, on a daily basis, from moment to moment. We reside in and are present in that creative-quantum consciousness, and if we commune with it, it is as if we are that consciousness. This is pure mysticism clothed in the modern language of quantum physics.

In quantum physics they call this consciousness not only 'non-local', which in other words is not time-space bound, identified with 'eternity', but also discontinuous. For many esoteric practitioners over the world, it has always been hard to maintain the state of 'non-being' as is wished for, particularly in the oriental traditions. Living in the world of time-space-movement implies that we cannot reside permanently in eternal consciousness (outside body and ego). If this was the case then we would be completely dysfunctional in life. Kabbalists have said for many centuries that the human being is a vehicle of Divinity, rather than an illusion that we must escape from as soon as possible.

Chapter 19: Wholeness

Kabbalah and quantum physics are about wholeness and integration, hinting at making life complete rather than dividing it up into separate parts, or excluding anything. Karma includes purpose, for we should not forget that by living in the natural world, we generate karma all the time. We are currently present in the world of action. Not only the world of physical action, but also mental, emotional, vital, and sensitive actions. Out of them, new effects arise that are in turn causes for other effects.

We may easily lose our sense of purpose in this vast and complicated human web of actions that we perform on a daily and nightly basis. Kabbalah and quantum physics both invite us to walk the way of awareness and conscious intent (Kavanah), so we may know more clearly what actions we establish within and through ourselves, into the world.

Purpose cannot arise out of coincidence nor out of some unconscious impulse. Although our purpose may call us from the deeper depths of the unconscious (like our maggid calling us), we must awaken to the call and what it tells us, in order to be able to follow it (diagrams A and B).

Four worlds in action
Quantum theory speaks about new paradigms that are inclusive, seeing the universe as eternal momentum where all is held in an unbreakable unity. Is the universe made up of energy and particle, where both are and are neither?

Yes, the universe, both is and isn't. Here we meet the mystical paradox about the Negative Veils in Kabbalah, where God is Nothing (Ain) and God is All (Ain Soph). The universe as a whole is a mirror of this mystical paradox, a mystical mirror that seems to reflect a twofold reality that is actually one.

This mirror is Daath, through which we can clearly see the complete reality as it is, coming to us, as a Divine revelation. Or it may come to us, as we generally see it, looking through 'a glass darkly', beholding the shadows of the light of reality. The diagram that we use in Kabbalah to portray the mirror of existence is the Tree of Life and Jacob's Ladder (diagram O).

There is a 'quantum reality' in Kabbalah; it is the twofold reality of 'being and becoming', metaphysically explained through the non-Sefira of Daath. Daath is the quantum point of transformation, located on the Daath of Yezirah and the Yesod of Briah: the place of the Holy Spirit.

Quantum consciousness is the consciousness of the mystic, 'who is and becomes' and who proclaims that she or he is 'in the world but not of this world'. Although quantum consciousness cannot be localised by our way of looking at time-space, we place it on the Tree, where there is indeed no reference to time and space, yet where such awareness is present in the world of time and space.

As we have said before, the quantum reality which is called 'the implicate order' by David Bohm and what we call Aziluth in Kabbalah is not outside of our relative reality.

Quantum intelligence (consciousness) comes into being through three successive worlds of development or emanation: creation, form, and action. The cosmos (higher world or Briah) is the medium of the quantum consciousness that awaits the Divine Will to emanate.

Through the worlds that step down into manifestation, quantum consciousness or Divinity reveals itself through Divine Intellect, emotion, and action. Again these are three lower worlds, beneath Aziluth. The creative reflection in the cosmos expresses itself through the stellar organization of the different archangels in the Kabbalah tradition. Archangels represent the essential, metaphysical principles that uphold the cosmos. They are the laws that govern the universe, guiding the higher, Divine influence into the lower vessels or worlds (diagram N).

In quantum philosophy, these principles could be explained as the scientific ideas that form the foundation of quantum physics. In a manner of speaking, some archangels are occupied with Wisdom and Understanding, the creative principles of Chocmah and Binah, that are called 'wave and particle' respectively in quantum terminology.

All that will come forth out of these cosmic parents is the descending order of the progressive development through entanglement (undivided hierarchy), non-locality (Eternity within the middle pillar or Kav of God), consciousness as the ground of being (all is derived out of consciousness or Divine potential), and 'collapse' or consequence of decision (free will). Without these cosmic principles, the lower worlds of form and matter would not be able to unfold. The cosmos is a medium for God's will, a vessel for the Divine wisdom. It is said that Divinity, the source and ground of all being (Aziluth), is the highest expression of love, what the Greeks called Agape.

Wisdom (Chocmah) is therefore the medium of love, while Understanding is the medium of Wisdom. Worlds below the Divine and the creative should be able to hold, sustain, and mirror the higher ones. Yezirah, the world of formation, is where the subtle astral and etheric forms serve as psychological vehicles for those Divine and creative influences. The mind is a vessel for the metaphysical (Spirit), and matter (Assiah) is a vessel or medium of the mind structures that contains the worlds above. These become worlds within worlds within worlds.

The mystery in Assiah lies within the Kabbalistic and quantum idea that Consciousness-Divinity is eventually expressed in matter. The Kingdom (Malkuth) is the place of the Shekinah (Holy Presence). In many esoteric and mystical traditions, the mystery is being transmitted that reality (Divinity) lies within. Reality is the totality and completeness of being. Once more, I emphasize the mystical work of the Kabbalist and quantum way alike: that we are seekers on the path of unity.

When we gradually remember that unity comes from within, we start to heal, as wholeness is healing in itself. This is exactly what the physical body does. It communicates and talks to us in a holistic way. The natural way the physical world talks is by means of completeness, coming from an interior awareness of physical existence, that God is immanent (Shekinah). Reality comes from inside, and so does healing. Breaking up the unity and wholeness is what we call being ill or sick. We feel broken and apart.

In chapters two and eight, we talked about the worlds and body existing as a hologram, thereby knowing itself in completeness through its individual parts. Although the separate parts do not express the totality of the whole, they reflect the whole as a separate unit.

For the natural world and the human being in particular, we can conclude that in the same way a part knows or experiences itself, so does the whole. If one part of us experiences a good thought, feeling of well-being, health, happiness, or wholeness, the whole being will feel this too.

As this is a principle of nature, the law that governs this wholeness through a holographic image does not make any distinction between 'good and bad thoughts or feelings'. Any part of us that feels depressed, sad, or angry will reflect this state of being in the complete mirror of our being. This beautifully explains the way that the Kabbalistic worlds mirror each other, but how within each world there are mirrors within mirrors—a Tree of Life within each Sefira.

The Kabbalist makes use of diagrams that present to us a picture of reality, namely the Tree of Life and Jacob's Ladder (diagrams A and G). Such a diagram should contain the whole of existence, describing and presenting a complete picture of who we are to the soul. All is about self-image. All is about identification.

It seems that God has willed it so, as the highest Divine expression in the world of Aziluth says to itself 'I am That I am'. God wishes to behold God in the mirror of existence. Existence may wake up to this mirror within and start to respond from the soul, who wishes out of existential desire to know itself. The Kabbalist remembers and rediscovers this image in the Tree of Life and Jacob's Ladder simultaneously, where our ideas, sense, and realizations about self are present.

From self-image comes identification. This little phrase is applied again and again every day, looking in the mirror of Yesod (Yezirah) and finding a sense of self. In truth, we do not find 'self' but a reflection of a fragment of that wholeness. To our understanding, the psychological mirror shows us who and what we are, leaving us identifying with what we behold in our personal mirror.

In the example of a reflection of beauty, one could identify oneself with compassion and forgiveness, but reflections do not distinguish between good and bad.

A mirror reflects, and that's it.

Meditation

Come to a state of meditation. Sit down or stand in this meditation. You can visualize the Tree of Life in front of you and/or place a diagram of the Tree of Life in front of you. Imagine that this Tree of Life shines and radiates towards you. It shines the light of truth. All that you truly were, are, and will become reflects like a mirror. You see yourself in this Tree of Life.

The diagram opposite you can do only one thing: reveal as a mirror who you are. Be still and receive what comes your way. Be ready to accept the truth that presents itself to you. After some time, integrate the experience by taking four deep breaths and making contact with your physical body.

Chapter 20: Yesod as a mirror

Yesod, with its shimmering quality of the moon, shines by means of who or what looks at it. If we feel sick or depressed, we may develop a growing identification with the sickness or depression. Who or what we see in the mirror is how we know ourselves. However, a reflection is not the reality, but only a reflection. The relevant question here should be: are you what you see, or is what you see a temporary reflection?

The function of the mirror is to reflect, in order to know what is and what is not. This means that we should not look indiscriminately at ourselves. Does the looker know who is looking?

Having spoken about the effect the observer or witness has on certain levels of reality in quantum measurement, we need to consider these questions seriously. A thought, a feeling, or an emotion has an equivalent in the chemical-electrical body, and it is quite dependent on how we look at the world and ourselves, to what degree we do shape our self-image and the image of the world around us (diagram J).

As a thought is fleeting, elusive, changeable, and short-lived, so are the substances that are released in the body. Are we also this fleeting person that comes and goes, passive towards the image that we see in the mirror of Yesod?

Memory is not only something we see, looking back into our personal history. Memory is a vital element in the process of how we consciously build our self-image. All thoughts, ideas, feelings, actions, and reflections of ourselves at this very moment contribute to how we see ourselves tomorrow. The more we behold our complete Tree of Life in our experience, the more we may become whole tomorrow. Be aware that memory can outlive any thought and physical cell in the body that was involved with your past experience.

All the cells of your body that were involved in a memory when you were stung by a wasp when you were little are gone and have been replaced several times, yet the memory lives on as long as the effects are still there in our reflections. A self-image can therefore be highly spiritual but it can also be a sick image. Addictions, fear, anxiety, pain are all examples of these distortions in memory and image.

The observer in Kabbalah and quantum teachings witnesses itself in the mirror. Being and becoming aware that there is a difference between the one who is looking and the image, the self grows in the knowledge that it is not only the image. Tifareth is the onlooker in the mirror of Yesod, occupying the Seat of Solomon on Jacob's Ladder, the place where the three lower worlds meet. We are conscious of three worlds in one mirror.

Besides the psychological mirror within the world of Yezirah we have an external mirror in Malkuth. This is the physical body we inhabit during our incarnation, but also the physical world around us. Together with the psychological Yesod, these are reflecting back at us constantly (day and night) where we are and who we are.

Without awakening from the spell that dances before our eyes, we remain in the enchantment (conditionings) of our own constructed world. From the quantum perspective, we could say that without the observer, who is the subject in any observation, we do not only 'see', but actively participate in what (object) is being observed. Besides this, if we do not observe beyond our known world and horizon or mirror, we will not participate in 'collapsing' (create through quantum consciousness) truly new and creative things.

To emphasize what we are discussing here, it is only through holding that position in the consciousness in the Seat of Solomon that we have access to (quantum) creativity. This arises out of the metaphysical law that worlds have to interlock, unite, and be realised in the awareness of the soul.

Body, mind, and Spirit are held together as one in a body of consciousness or a quantum body. Although we experience these bodies as separate and independent from each other, they are nevertheless one, interdependent and harmonious with each other (diagrams A and B).

Conclusion

Kabbalah has always been a tradition that teaches the way of unification. It is mystical teaching that does not guide souls to a transcendent state away from our relative existence. The way of Kabbalah is affirmative to life, inviting the Kabbalist to engage with all levels of existence and making them part of his or her own experience.

Science, as we have discussed in this book, may not have a mystical approach to life, yet is indeed also affirmative to our lives. The science of microbiology and quantum physics works towards integration, harmony, balance, and synthesis. Both Kabbalah and these sciences are concerned with the human being, how we move and find our place within the world. Furthermore, although most scientific thinking does not include consciousness within its philosophy, rejecting everything except rational and deductive thinking, the scientific disciplines discussed in this book do include consciousness. Not only this, they regard consciousness, as the Kabbalah does, as the ground of all being, or the metaphysical canvas upon which creation is being painted.

In the modern way of looking at microbiology, the interaction between cells and how they develop and generate a new consciousness and experience is an example of how consciousness is included. It is clear from this work that consciousness and the intelligence within all life are not limited to the brain, as we may have thought in the past. No, all existing parts of the human body are units of consciousness and intelligence. Even more, they communicate, interact, exchange, and make it possible to change fundamental behavior within and without the cell. The cell and its environment are in continuous communication with each other, bound together in a symmetrical system of life, where there is an order and purpose.

The Kabbalistic Tree of Life and the Jacob's Ladder show us the same natural order and a perpetual communication within the symmetrical diagrams of the Kabbalistic teaching. Within the cosmology of this Kabbalistic-scientific wisdom, we see that two worlds not only meet but blend together into a refined synthesis. Physics and metaphysics explain reality in two distinct and yet complementary ways. Quantum physics is no exception to this idea, as consciousness and the role of the observer play such a great part in giving shape to our reality. Kabbalah tells us that from the soul and free will, we may interact with the world in such a way that we influence the worldly processes.

There is an unbreakable connection between the soul and the world we are living in. Kabbalah and quantum physics makes this very clear. In this conclusion, I hope to encourage readers to use this knowledge and implications and become responsible creatures in this world. Responsibility from a spiritual point of view means that we start by being responsible for our own actions and what we bring forth into this world. This book shows us that we bring ourselves into the world continuously by all kinds of action, be it emotionally, psychologically, physically, or otherwise. We cause many things to be on a daily basis and most of it is unconsciously generated. Because of our innate ability to be a causation of reality, we should be aware of this faculty within us and consider the responsibilities of our actions.

Apart from this, the human being is obviously capable of performing much greater and even nobler works than we have considered possible until now. For the Kabbalist, the noblest of all work is the Great Work or the work of unity. It is clear that the sciences discussed in this book are also moving towards this Great Work.

We are all on our way, travelling and existing within that great mystery that might seem very far away, yet is closer than our own hearts. I wish you well on your journey.

Mike Bais, the Netherlands 2019